THE DOG
OWNER'S
HANDBOOK

THE DOG OWNER'S HANDBOOK

Graham Meadows and Elsa Flint

Foreword by Bruce Fogle

Reader's Digest

The Reader's Digest Association (Canada) Ltd.
Montreal

A Reader's Digest Book

Edited and designed by

Published in Canada in 2002 by

The Reader's Digest Association (Canada) Ltd.

1125 Stanley Street, Montreal, Quebec H3B 5H5

First published in 2001 by

New Holland (Publishers) Ltd

London • Cape Town • Sydney • Auckland

ISBN 0-88850-740-2

Managing Editors: Claudia Dos Santos (SA), Mari Roberts (UK)
Managing Art Editor: Peter Bosman
Editor: Gail Jennings
Design and Illustration: Steven Felmore
Picture Researcher: Sonya Meyer
Proofreader and Indexer: Sean Fraser
Production: Myrna Collins
Consultant (UK): Bas Hagreis

Reproduction by Disc Express (Cape) Pty Ltd
Printed and bound in Singapore by Tien Wah Press (Pte) Ltd
02 03 04 05/54321

Reader's Digest Books & Home Entertainment
Editorial Director: Deirdre Gilbert
Managing Editor: Philomena Rutherford
Art Director: John McGuffie

For information on this and other Reader's
Digest products or to request a catalogue,
please call our 24-hour Customer Service hotline at 1-800-465-0789.

You can also visit us on the World Wide Web
at http://www.readersdigest.ca

Reader's Digest and the Pegasus logo are registered trademarks of The Reader's Digest
Association Inc.

**National Library of Canada
Cataloguing in Publication Data**

Meadows, Graham
    The dog owner's handbook

Includes index
ISBN 0-88850-740-2

    I. Dogs. I Flint, Elsa. II. Title.

SF427M42 2002   636.7'0887
C2001-900336-6

page 1
The German Shepherd Dog is particularly intelligent and has
highly developed senses, which makes it easy to train.

page 2
The Golden Cocker Spaniel is a strong, independent breed, and
usually cannot tolerate being teased by children.

pages 4 and 5
The Golden Retriever is an excellent swimmer, and in the 19th
century used to work as 'crew' on Newfoundland fishing
boats, helping to bring heavy nets to shore.

There are many different dog breeds, each with particular characteristics, traits and even aptitudes. It is the duty of all pet owners to choose a dog that will fit in with their lifestyle and the environment they are able to provide for it. Large breeds, such as those depicted above, require much space, as well as training and regular daily exercise.

CONTENTS

Generally, Labrador Retrievers have a calm disposition and are intelligent, hard working and reliable. These positive qualities make them eminently suitable for training as guide dogs for the blind.

FOREWORD
The essence of dog-ownership

Dogs are not changing – we are. Not so long ago a dog was considered 'part of the furniture'. Today it is an active part of the family, a best buddy, a listening friend and a helping paw.

From the time canines first entered human homes, emotion played a role in our alliance with them. My observation during 30 years as a practising veterinarian is that emotional ties play an increasingly prominent role as our relationships with pet dogs are becoming progressively complex. And frequently we get all it wrong. Let me explain.

I accept that dogs and people share similar emotions. Elation, fear, tranquillity, anxiety, contentment, anger and even love are feelings that dogs share with us.

But your dog does not understand everything you say. It recognises a selection of words, and can determine your mood from the inflection in your voice. Dogs can read your body language, but they are unable to understand language as we do. Since we treat our dogs like members of the family, we tend to think of them as human and treat them accordingly. But we often expect too much of them.

We should never expect them to do more than their evolutionary status as highly sociable pack animals permits.

Emotion also plays a significant role in a relatively new area of veterinary care: geriatrics. This, together with medical genetics, is the burgeoning growth area in veterinary medicine. Pharmaceutical companies have discovered a vigorous demand for medicines that control age-related behaviour disorders such as disorientation, joint pain and incontinence. Food manufacturers formulate diets that ease the strain on the kidneys or hearts of the elderly. Due to our increased emotional investment in them, we want our dogs to live as long as possible, and advances in geriatric medicine mean that vets can now prolong the lives of pets.

Understanding where dogs have come from, their natural behaviour and our relationship with them all form the basis for what comes next: living with us. Whatever the relationship, our dogs depend on us for good nutrition, proper training, disease prevention and physical and emotional care. Read and learn. I hope you get as much pleasure from your canine companion as my family and I have had from all of ours.

Cordially,
Bruce Fogle

DOGS AND PEOPLE

From wild origins to domestication

If you have ever thought that Alaskan Malamutes and German Shepherd dogs look very much like wolves, you are pretty close to the mark. Despite many opinions as to exactly how and where our modern dog breeds originated, there is very strong evidence (DNA analysis) that domesticated wolves were their common distant ancestors.

Dogs and wolves are both classified as members of the family *Canidae* and share similar characteristics:

- forty-two teeth
- fifty to 52 vertebrae (seven cervical, 13 thoracic, seven lumbar, three sacral, 20–22 coccygeal)
- a circularly contracting iris
- a similar sense of smell
- similar diseases
- similar behaviour
- an exceptional sense of direction
- nocturnal habits
- a propensity to dig
- gestation of nine weeks
- their puppies' eyes open at about two weeks of age.

Wolves (*Canis lupus*), also known as grey wolves, are found only in the northern hemisphere, throughout Europe, North America and Asia. Wolves in the far north vary in colour:

animals in a single pack may be black, grey-brown, and white. Those in warmer climates are less aggressive, smaller, more uniform in colour, often yellowish-fawn or grizzled grey-brown like the domestic dog (*Canis familiaris*).

Wolves and people

We can understand how and why an association developed between wolves and people if we compare their lifestyles during the period of history (between 15,000 and 60,000 years ago) that led to the wolf's domestication.

Humans were semi-nomadic hunter-gatherers. They lived in groups, used natural shelters such as caves and made forays to hunt for food. They had leaders upon whose skill or experience the rest of the group relied. Hunting required physical strength and was primarily the task of males; cooking food and rearing children was largely the domain of females.

Wolves also lived together in extended family groups, or packs, within which there was a distinct hierarchy and a pack leader. They made use of what natural shelter was available,

---

ABOVE: The grey wolf – ancestor of many North American dog breeds.

TOP: Dog ownership brings with it a number of therapeutic benefits, not only the joy of companionship. Dog owners suffer less stress, are less aggressive and judgmental and live longer.

and like humans they also made forays to hunt. Females gave birth to, and reared, their cubs, and for much of the time relied on the strength and ability of the males to protect them and provide food.

Because wolves and humans were hunters, they almost certainly competed with each other from time to time. The wolf's acute sense of smell helped it to track down its prey, and humans may have taken advantage of this by finding wolves that had made a kill, driving them away and taking over the carcass. Wolves probably followed humans who were hunting and picked up any scraps that were left behind.

As time went by, humans developed a distinct advantage over their canine competitors: the ability to use primitive weapons that made their hunting more effective. A better supply of food meant a more stable lifestyle, and humans began to spend more time in semi-permanent encampments.

Bones from wolf-like dogs have been found in excavations of human encampments dating from 30,000 to 60,000 years ago. They were almost certainly not pets, but semi-wild animals killed by the human inhabitants for food, or had been attracted to the encampments to scavenge on food scraps. Humans may have encouraged such scavengers, for the wolves' superior sense of smell and hearing would have enabled them to detect approaching predators, such as bears or lions, much sooner than the human residents.

Early humans probably made use of the wolf's hunting and scenting ability, and the protection it offered, in much the same way that we use dogs today. In return the wolves obtained some food, and by remaining close to encampments also received a certain amount of protection, for most large predators would not venture too close to humans.

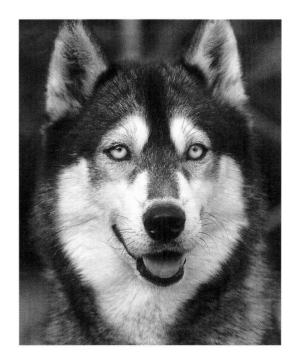

ABOVE: The Alaskan Malamute bears a close resemblance to its grey wolf ancestors.
TOP: Grey wolves in a wild environment. Today, grey wolves are found only in Canada, parts of the United States, Russia, and pockets of Eastern Europe.

The process of domestication

Over a period of time, wolves living close to humans became more relaxed and sociable towards them. Both dogs and humans discovered mutual benefits from this loose used the sub-species of wolf that occurred in their particular area, but as humans migrated there came a great deal of interbreeding. Four subspecies of wolf had a particular influence on the development of our modern dog breeds:

Patterns of dominant and submissive behaviour in wolves

Dominant behaviour		Submissive behaviour	
Dominant pose	Stiff, tall stance Ears up or forward Tail up or out	Submissive posture	Crouched posture Ears flat and tail tucked in Forehead smooth Pulling corners of mouth back ('grinning') Licking or extruding the tongue Lowering and averting the gaze
Feet on	Dominant places its forelegs across the shoulders of a subordinate	Submissive arched posture	Back very arched and neck curved down and to the side. Head low, muzzle extended up Tail tucked in and ears flat Lifting hind leg while dropping to the ground, exposing the inguinal region
Muzzle pin	Dominant either bites or grabs subordinate's muzzle, forcing it to the ground and keeping it there	Submissive sit	Sitting back, tucking chin into chest, sometimes pawing at the dominant and averting gaze
Stand across	Dominant stands stiffly across the forequarters of a prone subordinate		

association, which gradually became closer and led to the process of domestication. One of the key factors in this process was the wolf's natural instinct to obey a pack leader, and the ability of humans to fulfil that role. Caught when very young, a wild wolf cub was likely to obey its human master and be tamed.

Domestication was a gradual process that occurred during very similar time periods in Europe, Asia and North America – around 10–15,000 years ago. Initially humans

○ The Indian wolf probably gave rise to the ancestors of the Dingo and Asian Pariah Dog. The Dingo's ancestors moved eastwards with human migration, and eventually became isolated in Australia.

○ From the Chinese wolf evolved breeds such as the Pekingese and Chow Chow.

○ The grey wolf was a major source of North American breeds, such as the Eskimo Dog and Alaskan Malamute.

ABOVE: This Canadian grey wolf displays typical dominance aggression as it protects its food.

○ European wolves were probably involved in the development of breeds such as the various Shepherd Dogs, Spitz types and Terriers.

The development of dog types

The process of selection and refinement lasted many thousands of years, and was based on the human needs for food, protection and companionship. Dogs had an excellent sense of smell and were faster and more agile than men, so they proved to be valuable allies when it came to tracking and hunting the animals on which humans relied for their food, skins and fur. Dogs also proved useful for watch and guard duty, and for killing the vermin that were attracted to the food in the human encampments. Some wolves proved better at certain tasks than others, and human selection gradually produced different types of dog.

During the Neolithic Age, which started about 8,000 years ago, humans learned to grow crops. They also domesticated and farmed goats, sheep and cattle, so they selected dogs to provide a further service: herding.

By choosing their primitive domestic dogs for different purposes, humans incidentally selected for particular characteristics. Among these were temperament, body shape and body size.

It is suggested that in selecting for temperament they chose animals that were playful, outgoing and showed little aggression towards people, yet readily barked at the appearance of intruders. These traits were consistent with the behaviour of young animals, and over a period of time resulted in an adult population that retained many 'puppy' characteristics. Scientifically, this is referred to as 'neoteny'.

In developing a dog type, body shape and size were clearly important. Dogs required to hunt fast-running prey needed speed and agility, and therefore a relatively light, fine-boned body with long legs and a flexible spine. Large, strong dogs were required to hunt prey such as gazelles, but dogs used for hunting hares could be smaller. A dog whose job was to catch rats or dig out a rabbit's burrow needed quickness and agility, and thus a compact body and short legs.

A dog required to haul loads needed to be strong and sturdy, and bigger to support the large masses of muscle.

Temperament was also an important factor. A large dog developed for guard duties had to have the courage to face an intruder and display aggression. An equally large dog developed to haul loads, a job in which it regularly came into contact with strangers, had to be trusting and remain calm. A small ratting dog needed to retain its innate hunting instinct so that it would immediately snap at vermin.

Early domestic dogs

The characteristics that people demanded of their dogs varied in different parts of the world, depending on the environment, climate and human lifestyle. People living in the far north needed dogs that could haul loads and withstand extremely cold conditions, and archaeological finds in North America show that 7,500 years ago there were already dogs weighing about 23kg (50lb) that were very similar to the Eskimo Dog of today. They had shorter muzzles than grey wolves, but almost certainly retained their ancestor's stamina and strength.

In Asia and Europe, dogs derived from Indian and Eurasian wolves were also being bred to do particular types of work, such as hunting. Greyhounds are depicted in Egyptian frescoes dated around 5,000 years ago, and later, smaller hounds appeared that were similar to the Pharaoh Hound and Ibizan Hound we know today.

ABOVE: The Dingo arrived in Australia about 4,000 years ago, the descendent of the Indian wolf – it has never been fully domesticated and is seldom kept as a companion.
TOP: The ancient Egyptian dog-god Anubis, the god of the underworld.

Another modern breed whose ancestors are discernible around that time is the Saluki, while a palace dog kept by the ancient Pharaohs in Egypt about 2,000 BC is similar to the present-day Basenji.

Sight hounds and scent hounds

Most of the early dogs were hounds, which suggests that a chief objective in early dog-breeding programmes was to develop varieties suitable for hunting. The development of these varieties varied according to the part of the world in which their human owners lived.

In Egypt, animal scents quickly disseminated on the hot, dry sands. Most of the early hounds therefore relied on their vision to identify their quarry from a distance before running it down; hence the development of 'sight' or 'gaze' hounds, from which breeds such as the Afghan and Saluki were developed. These animals also needed speed (long legs and a long supple body) and stamina (a large lung capacity within a deep chest).

Scents lingered for much longer in the cooler and moister environments of forests and woodlands – conditions common in Greece and Italy. Thick undergrowth prevented dogs from being able to follow their quarry by sight, so they needed to be able to track it by scent over long distances. These 'scent' hounds were physically different from 'sight' hounds. They had shorter legs and more compact, muscular bodies, and were built for endurance. We know that such dogs existed several thousand years ago.

Spitz dogs

These dogs have a characteristic curly tail and are represented by modern breeds such as the Siberian Husky, Samoyed and Chow Chow. There is evidence to suggest that dogs of this type were widely spread throughout the world. In China, the ancestors of the Chow Chow are featured on Han Dynasty pottery statues dated at 200 BC.

A northern connection came a thousand years later: the Vikings brought Spitz-type dogs with them when they invaded and settled parts of England.

Other early domestic dog types

In China and Tibet other ancestral dog types were being developed, as pets and guard dogs, and these gave rise to short-nosed breeds such as the Pekingese, Lhasa Apso, Shih Tzu, Tibetan Spaniel, Tibetan Terrier and Japanese Chin.

In the Mediterranean region at least five or six distinctly different dog types were already in existence by Roman times. They included small dogs not unlike today's Dachshund, fast hunting dogs similar to the Greyhound, and large, heavy, guard dogs rather like the Mastiff. There were short-nosed and long-nosed dogs, similar to today's Pug and Borzoi. In Britain the Celtic Hounds, forerunners of the Irish Wolfhound, were already established before the Roman invasion.

ABOVE: The English Springer Spaniel was specifically developed to pick up game birds.

TOP: The Egyptian Pharaoh Hound spread to Europe after the Roman invasion of Egypt around 2,000 years ago.

The arrival of the 'pet' dog

As time went by, more types of dog were developed. Dogs that could hunt by both sight and scent proved useful as all-purpose hunters, and from them were developed the smaller 'earth' dogs, now known as terriers. Their name comes from the word 'terra', Latin for earth. They were short-legged, tough and hardy, expert at detecting and catching smaller quarry and an invaluable aid in keeping down the vermin that thrived in most areas of human habitation.

Dogs required for herding cattle and sheep needed to be agile and intelligent, and retain many of the characteristics of their wolf ancestors, who performed similar tasks during a hunt when singling out the weaker animals.

Larger and heavier Mastiff-type dogs were developed to pull loads, protect herds and flocks from dangerous predators such as wild bears or wolves, or guard property against both animals and humans.

The bond that exists between most of today's owners and their dogs is not new. Two thousand years ago a shepherd in Turkey probably had similar feelings about his working dog as a Canadian, British or Australian farmer does today. But while many people would have felt the need for a dog's companionship in those early days, few could have afforded to keep and feed a dog that did not work for its living.

Pet dogs were largely the province of the wealthy. In China and Japan, 'toy' dogs were kept by the emperors and

TOP: The meat of this black-tongued breed, the Chow Chow, was once regarded as a delicacy in Manchuria and Mongolia, and its fur was used for clothing. Today the Chow Chow is a real one-person dog, with a tendency to be aggressive with strangers.

15

their courts, and it was only when European travellers began to visit those countries that many of the breeds were 'discovered' and brought back to Europe and England. By AD 500 the Bichon family of dogs was established, giving rise to today's Bichon Frise and possibly the Lowchen. Various types of small dog were also developed in monasteries, where their roles ranged from companion to watchdog.

With the passing of the centuries, more of today's breeds took shape. In AD 1300 the Black Hound, forerunner of the Bloodhound, was established in Britain, while in Europe and Asia herding dogs were developing – among them the ancestors of the Hungarian Puli and Komondor.

Perhaps as many as three-quarters of today's dog breeds were developed during the last 300 years or so. Improvement in the range and accuracy of firearms resulted in the introduction and refinement of many of today's sporting breeds, while increased affluence led to more interest in general purpose and toy dogs.

By the beginning of the 20th century the development was almost complete, and most of the refinements since then have been cosmetic rather than functional.

Dog breeds and kennel clubs

Today there are hundreds of breeds (some encyclopaedias list more than 400), many of them recognised only in their country of origin. Breed standards are established, which enables breeders and judges to select progeny that come closest to the required characteristics, therefore ensuring their continuation. To gain recognition, a breed must have clearly identifiable characteristics that are passed between generations; these become the basis for the breed's establishment.

Many countries have their own Kennel Club or similar organisation that controls and monitors the registration and showing of pedigree dogs. It recognises particular breeds for show purposes and classifies them into groups based on similarities of use or characteristics.

TOP: One of the world's most popular dogs, the Pointer was originally bred as a hunting companion due to its excellent sight and sense of smell, coupled with intelligence and a keen ability to learn.

The number of groups, their names and the breeds within them are not consistent between countries. There is some agreement about four of the groups (Toys, Gundogs/Sporting Dogs, Terriers and Hounds), but not about any others. Some countries, such as Canada, have separate groups for working dogs and herding dogs, and what we name non-sporting dogs are called utility or Spitz breeds (dogs with the characteristic appearance of a Spitz or primitive breed: tail curled over the back and pricked ears) elsewhere.

Because each country has its own method of classifying dog breeds, the Fédération Cynologique Internationale (FCI) was formed to rationalise the differences. It divides breeds into 10 groups, using its own classification system: Sheep Dogs and Cattle Dogs (other than Swiss Cattle Dogs); Pinschers and Schnauzer type, Molossian type, Swiss Mountain and Cattle dogs; large and medium-sized Terriers; Dachshunds; Spitz and primitive types; Scenthounds and related breeds; Pointing Dogs; Companion and Toy Dogs; Sighthounds; and Retrievers, Flushing Dogs and Water Dogs. At the time of writing it had registered 331 breeds.

Member countries of the FCI (78 at time of writing) define their own breed standards but submit them to the FCI for international recognition.

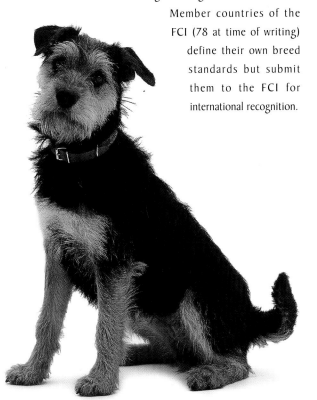

Cross-breeds and mongrels

This chapter would not be complete without a brief mention of those lovable canines of mixed or unknown ancestry. Cross-breeds are animals of known parentage from two different breeds. Mongrels are of unknown ancestry. Endowed with what scientists term hybrid vigour, they often (but not always) combine some of the more desirable characteristics of their ancestors. They may not be officially recognised, but they still bring joy and comfort to millions of people.

Sadly, they are also the main product of uncontrolled breeding and account for the majority of unwanted puppies, or dogs 'dumped' by their owners, that end up in animal shelters. Despite efforts to educate owners and discourage indiscriminate breeding, this worldwide problem continues.

A special bond

These days pet animals are one of the many factors that make up what we call quality of life. During the last 20 years, numerous studies have confirmed the psychological and medical benefits of pet ownership. These benefits have also become a basis for programmes based on animal-assisted activities, also referred to as 'pet-facilitated therapy' and 'animal-facilitated therapy'. In these programmes, interactions with animals are used to assist humans with physical or psychological problems.

In industrialised societies increasing affluence, a falling birth rate and looser family ties have resulted in pets playing a more important psychological role. More couples are choosing not to have any children, or to have them later in life after the female partner has established a career, and for many of these people a pet becomes an important member of the family. But regardless of your family status, owning a dog is likely to provide you with some important benefits.

Companionship

For four out of five dog owners the most important feature of owning a dog is the company it provides. Companionship may mean simply having the dog around or the dog may be a working companion or used for a specific task.

ABOVE: Cross-breeds and mongrels account for the majority of dogs in almost every country in the world. Where possible, before you select a mongrel puppy, observe the temperament of its mother.

For many of us a dog acts as a safeguard against loneliness; it becomes a partner and a friend in whom we can confide. If you think you are unusual in talking to your dog as if it were another human being, don't worry. You are not unusual at all. Most of us behave in a similar way.

As well as talking to our dogs, we instinctively use methods of communication that we would use with members of our own species. To console our dogs, for example, we use standard 'primate gestures' such as stretching out our hands and patting them, pursing and smacking our lips and uttering soothing noises, although men are generally less demonstrative in this respect than women.

Comfort

A subtle aspect of animal companionship is the physical proximity or nearness of an animal to its owner. The mere fact that our dog is in the same room as us produces a feeling of comfort, and the more attached we are to our dog the closer it may be allowed to sleep to us at night. Some dogs share their owner's bed, while others are made to sleep outside the home in their own kennel or shed.

Comfort may also come from direct physical contact, or simply from the affection that it displays towards you.

Relaxation

Your dog will help you relax. It has been conclusively demonstrated that a person in a state of tension shows a slowing of the heart rate and a drop in blood pressure when their pet comes on the scene. Owning a pet can be an important stress-management practice for people with high stress levels in their work.

Physical security and protection

An increase in crime in some societies has resulted in more people keeping watchdogs or guard dogs as additional protection for themselves and their property. In these cases there is a trend towards keeping the larger, potentially more aggressive breeds such as the Doberman, German Shepherd Dog or Rottweiler, and other breeds that have been specifically developed for guarding, such as the Neapolitan Mastiff and Dogue de Bordeaux.

But it is not just the size or potential aggressiveness of a dog that is important. For many of us, our feeling of security lies in the knowledge that the animal will detect and react to a stranger or intruder long before we can, and this gives us more time to react to such a situation. For this reason many owners of small dogs feel just as secure with their pet as they would with a large, specially trained guard dog.

Emotional security

In addition to physical protection, a dog can also provide us with psychological protection. For example, it can give us

TOP: The Golden Retriever is an affection-demanding breed – and with their exceptional patience towards children, they nearly always receive the affection they so enjoy.

the emotional security to face or overcome irrational fears, such as a fear of the dark or anxiety at being left alone.

If you are doing something in a strange environment, or meeting strangers, having your dog with you can enable you to carry out your tasks more effectively or communicate better. For example, one sociological study into human behaviour showed that people interviewed by a researcher accompanied by her dog generally felt more comfortable and relaxed than those interviewed without the dog present.

Helping to establish new friendships

There is plenty of evidence to show that people who like dogs are more likely to like other people, and are more socially interactive. So if you own a dog you are probably very good at establishing new human friendships.

Dogs certainly act as ice breakers for contact between humans. Take your dog for a walk and it is quite possible that a usually reserved neighbour or even a total stranger will stop and comment on its appearance or behaviour. Dogs also act as an important link between the young and the old.

Self-fulfilment and self-esteem

We all need to feel good about ourselves. Many of us achieve this through success in our family relationships, work, sport or other recreational activities. Others achieve it through reflected glory by owning a dog that is an object of prestige. It may be a rare or unusual breed, a winner in the show ring or an obedience or agility champion.

For some of us the mere responsibility of caring for another living creature can result in a sense of self-worth, and by doing it correctly we may be rewarded by the approval of other people.

Aesthetic satisfaction

Your dog doesn't have to be a show winner in order to give you pleasure. If you have chosen it for its character and appearance, then every time you look at it you will feel good.

An aid to leisure activities

Dogs are an important part of our leisure experience. Dogs like to play, and they stimulate us to play with them. This helps us to relax and develop a more active zest for life, diverting us from the comparative drudgery of family chores or work. For many of us merely looking after a dog, such as feeding, grooming and exercising it, can become a leisure activity in itself.

Benefits to children

About two out of three families that own a dog also have children. We might ask why parents coping with a growing family would want to adopt another, non-human member,

The sensitive Rough Collie (**TOP RIGHT**) grows deeply attached to its owner and makes a good guard dog, while the West Highland White Terrier (**TOP LEFT**) is excitable and loves attention.

Research has shown that children will often confide in the family dog, spending just as much time talking to it about the day's successes and failures as they do with their brothers or sisters. When their parents or siblings aren't around, the dog acts as a substitute. It is interesting to note that the children most likely to develop social skills and empathy with other people are those who talk intimately and at length with their pets and their grandparents.

Emotional support

If your family has suffered the loss of a loved one, or a teenager is going through a particularly difficult period in his or her life, your dog can provide much-needed emotional support at such a critical time.

A responsible attitude, better housekeeping

Those of us who have had to put up with muddy paws through a long and wet winter may wonder how owning a dog could possibly contribute to improved hygiene, yet it has been shown that families with pets are generally more hygiene conscious than those without.

and the answer is not entirely clear. Many of us think that having a pet dog will help teach our children responsibility: that a child who learns to care for a pet is more likely to have a caring attitude towards fellow humans.

There is also an educational value. If our children learn about a dog's body processes such as sexual maturity and reproduction, and how to cope with its health problems or illnesses, they may be better prepared for their own experiences later in life. The life span of a pet dog is approximately 10–15 years, and may match the period during which our children are growing to maturity. The life of our dog might help to teach them about growing up, learning, old age, suffering and death. Caring for it during that lifetime may teach them some valuable 'parenting' skills.

The presence of a pet dog in your household can help your children to overcome anxiety, control aggression, develop self-awareness and deal with life's problems.

ABOVE: This Airedale puppy should grow up to be tough, strong, stubborn and intensely faithful.

TOP: The Labrador Retriever is one of the world's most popular breeds: a real family animal.

Therapeutic value

Your dog will probably bring you plenty of other benefits. Statistically you are likely to:

○ live longer
○ have lower blood pressure
○ be in less danger of heart attacks if you are prone to them
○ have better motivation and be more purposeful
○ be less egocentric and more supportive of others
○ suffer less stress and gain more relief of tension
○ be emotionally stronger and less likely to become depressed
○ be less aggressive
○ be less judgmental of other people's faults or afflictions.

Benefits to the elderly

Dogs can be of special benefit to elderly people, who often fail to feed themselves properly. Feeding their dog stimulates them to eat, too, and their dog provides them with company while they are eating. Many elderly people are not allowed to take their dog with them when they enter a retirement home, yet there are many valid reasons why they should be allowed to do so.

Failed human-dog relationships

Not all dog-owner relationships are a success. Perhaps as many as one in five fail, so if your first experience in dog ownership has not been a happy one, you are not alone. Make an effort to analyse the reasons for your experience. Your vet may be able to help identify the causes.

A dog may become a problem because:

○ it was wrongly selected, and doesn't fit in to your environment/family/lifestyle
○ it wasn't trained properly by you or allowed to socialise properly with other animals in the household
○ there was an inherent problem in the dog's genetic make-up.

If you can identify the reasons for the problems you experienced with your previous dog, and eliminate those problems, then do try again. Owning a dog can indeed add to the quality of your life.

TOP: Elderly people living alone who are dog owners have been shown to be more motivated and purposeful than those in similar circumstances without dogs.

A NEW DOG FOR YOU

Selecting your companion

If you have previously owned a dog and experienced the unique bond that can develop between you, then you will know that ownership involves an ongoing responsibility and long-term commitment, consideration for others and a responsible attitude towards society. You will also already know that, properly treated, a dog can prove a loyal and affectionate friend and give its owner many years of love and devotion.

When choosing a new dog, don't let your heart rule your head. Be aware of the size (height, length and weight) to which a puppy may grow, the amount of food it will eat, the grooming and exercise it will need, the temperament it might have, the possible health problems that might arise and its possible life span.

Before deciding to get a dog as a pet, whether it is for the first time or as a replacement, ask yourself the following important questions:

What do you expect from the dog?

- Do you want your dog to become a member of the family, sharing your home and your life?
- Do you want it to act as a watchdog to warn you when strangers arrive, or to guard your property when you are away? Most dogs, regardless of their size, will sound an alarm when something strange occurs, or if somebody appears on your premises, and in most cases they provide enough warning and protection. If you want a dog of a breed that is an ideal guard dog, it will require proper training and handling. If you don't have the expertise to do this properly, don't get one.
- Do you want it to be successful in shows or other competition, and if so, why?
- List all your expectations, and then try to choose the type of dog that might fulfil them.

To whom will it belong?

Be sure you know who will be responsible for your dog and look after it. Involve all members of the family in the decision-making process, but make sure that one, committed person has the overall responsibility and will act as leader of the pack.

ABOVE: It is important that only one person is the official 'owner' of a dog, and acts as the 'pack leader'.
TOP: Before you blithely give a dog as a gift, consider whether the receiver is able or willing to offer the commitment, environment and stability needed by a dog.

Do you have enough knowledge? If you are a first-time dog owner, make sure you know what you are taking on. A dog needs much more than feeding, exercise and grooming. It needs training and regular health care throughout its life, and may need special care when it is old.

Do you have enough time? You will need to devote a lot of time to bringing up and training a puppy, and to giving a juvenile and adult dog the companionship it needs. Over a period of years you will spend many thousands of hours training and generally caring for the animal.

Do you have enough commitment? You must be prepared to lose a certain amount of freedom, and commit for 10–15 years, perhaps longer. You may have done this once already, but are you capable of doing it again?

Can you give it the right environment? Is your home large enough for the type of dog you would like? Are there areas nearby where it can be adequately exercised? Can you keep it confined to your property and prevent it from roaming the neighbourhood?

Can you afford it? Apart from any initial cost of purchasing a dog and accessories, there are ongoing costs for food, annual vaccinations and health care, and possibly for neutering. There may be registration fees, and costs involved in fencing your garden, attending obedience-training classes, or kennelling the dog while you are away on holiday.

Can you offer the dog a stable home? Are your circumstances likely to change in the foreseeable future? Is the owner of the dog likely to go away to university, move cities or travel overseas for any length of time? Is the proposed owner elderly or infirm, or likely to suffer health problems that might affect his or her ability to care for a dog?

Which sex will you choose? Decide if you want a male or female, and if you will consider neutering either sex. Bitches are usually smaller than males, more manageable

ABOVE: You may be tempted to buy a puppy (or two) because of its cuteness, but remember that when it grows up, it will need more than simply feeding and exercise: it will need training, regular health care and special care when it is old.

and more easily trained. Unless they are spayed, they will have an oestrus cycle ('come into season' or 'be in heat') every six months.

Is a dog the right species? Think about this very carefully. Would a cat or some other domestic pet be more suitable? Assess all your options before committing yourself.

Integrating a new dog with one you already own

You may already own a dog, perhaps one that is getting on in years, and wish to bring another one into the household. Whether this will cause problems or not will depend on a number of factors, including the ages of the dogs and how you go about integrating them.

The two dogs will need to establish their own hierarchy within the household – which one is dominant and which subordinate. They may do this with little or no incident – a young puppy, for example, will usually defer to an older, naturally more dominant dog. There may be problems, though, if the new dog is an adolescent and decides to become the dominant dog, and your other dog objects. (For more details, see pp71–2, Aggression between dogs in the same household.)

Selecting a dog

It is important that you match your dog to your individual circumstances and your ability to look after it properly.

An old adage states that 'there are no bad dogs, merely bad owners'. In many cases it holds true, although some dogs have inherited temperamental problems. Most so-called dog problems really are owner problems, caused by a mismatch of the breed (with its needs and temperament) and the owner (with his or her temperament and lifestyle).

Such a mismatch between dog and owner can result in a dog living a socially deprived life in an entirely unsuitable environment. Under such circumstances, behaviour problems are likely to occur.

If a terrier, whose innate instinct is to dig, is left alone in a small garden while its owners are out, it will probably wreck the flowerbeds and/or dig its way out under the fence. If a dog that craves company has to watch its owner depart for work, then spend the next eight hours alone, it is very likely to suffer from separation anxiety.

People wanting a dog for protection often choose a large dog of a 'guarding' breed. In many cases it is the dog's size and strength that result in it becoming a problem. If they are unwilling or unable to train it properly and control the dog when walking it on a lead, the owners often resort to leaving it to exercise itself in the garden, which is usually far too small. Feeling enclosed and frustrated, the dog becomes bored and starts to dig holes, whine, howl and bark at anything or anyone that passes by. If the garden is fenced, it will find the smallest of gaps to peer through, then

ABOVE: This young Alaskan Malamute male puppy will grow to a rather formidable size.
TOP: Retired racing Greyhounds, such as this one, make excellent companions; however, they do tend to chase anything that moves and may need careful retraining.

bark madly the moment anyone passes by, frightening them out of their wits and giving the dog exactly the reward it needs to repeat the process. If this behaviour goes unchecked, it may become aggressive and a potential danger to visitors to its home.

Pure-bred or mongrel?

There are thousands of mongrel dogs (also called mixed breeds or cross-breeds) in dog shelters and pet shops, waiting for a loving home. Many of them will make ideal companions, and the 'hybrid vigour' that comes from their mixed (often unknown) parentage may ensure that they have a healthy constitution and are less likely to suffer from any inherited or breed-specific defects.

The main disadvantage in selecting one is that you don't know what breeds are in its parentage. You may be able to get some idea from its shape and size, but you will have far less information about its likely temperament than if you select a pure-bred animal.

If you do decide to opt for such a dog, try to insist on a trial period of at least one month.

Adopting an older dog

You may hear of an adult dog that needs a new home. Check the reasons for this. They may be genuine: for example, a family may be emigrating and unable to take the dog with them, or the owner may have become ill or has moved into a much smaller home, and can no longer look after the dog. On the other hand, if the owner is parting with the dog because of behaviour problems, you may be better off looking elsewhere. Keep in mind that some problems are more easily surmounted than others, so find

ABOVE: A mixed-breed can make an ideal companion, although it is wise to take it home for a trial period of a month or so, to discover its true temperament.

out why the dog is available for adoption before making a decision. In older dogs, aggression or a propensity for running away aren't easily corrected and you would be wise to continue your search. However, owners who are absent from home all day may simply be parting with a pet because it becomes distressed if left alone for long periods. Such a dog may be perfect for your household. Or perhaps the owners have found caring for the dog too onerous. Certain breeds, for example, require professional grooming every three months: Airedales and Fox Terriers must be stripped, Poodles need to be clipped. Would this also be too onerous for you?

Some Greyhounds become available for adoption when their racing days are over. These are usually docile and fit well into a family environment, but because they have been trained to chase a moving, furry object, they can be a danger to certain household or neighbourhood pets.

Selecting a breed

If you already own, or have owned, a dog of a particular breed, you may decide to choose that same breed again.

On the other hand, you may have owned a mixed-breed or mongrel, and want to try a pure-bred dog. In that case, remember that breeds come in many different shapes, sizes and temperaments, and choosing one to suit you requires careful consideration.

Think about the following in relation to the breeds you are considering:

- the size of dog you want
- the purpose for which you want it: companionship, show, work, obedience training or as a watchdog
- your knowledge and experience of dogs, and ability to handle particular breeds
- the strength of your preferred breed, and whether you can physically handle it
- the type of home in which you live, and the amount of indoor and outdoor space
- the type of environment in which you live: urban, semi-rural or rural
- the number and type of people who live in your home. Some breeds are not so tolerant of children; others are too boisterous with elderly or infirm people
- the amount of human companionship you can offer
- the amount of time you can devote to feeding and grooming

ABOVE: The Lhasa Apso was originally bred in Tibet as an indoor watchdog, kept by Buddhist monks.
TOP: If you don't want your personal grooming equipment to be snatched by your puppy, don't allow it to play with its own grooming tools.

- the amount of exercise you can give the dog
- the amount of training you can give it. Some breeds require firm handling and more advanced training from a professional.
- your climate. Short-faced breeds (such as the Bulldog) sometimes suffer from breathing problems in a hot climate. For subtropical or tropical climates consider short-coated, long-nosed breeds. Breeds with long thick coats benefit from seasonal changes to assist coat shedding. Cold climate breeds include the Chow Chow, Spitz, Samoyed, Norwegian Elkhound, and Newfoundland.

If you know how and why a breed was developed you are more likely to understand the nature and instinctive behaviour of the dog you hope to own.

To identify the breed that may best suit you, take the time to read about each of the breeds you fancy. Talk to your vet, because he or she deals with different breeds every day and can help you to select a suitable breed. Remember that there can be enormous variations between individuals within a particular breed, and it is essential to carefully assess every animal that you inspect.

Choosing a dog breeder

Responsible breeders aim to produce mentally and physically healthy dogs that embody the characteristics demanded by the agreed breed standard. They also try to ensure that puppies go to owners who will properly care for them. They vet their customers and their homes before selling to them, provide clear and concise information about their breed, recommend suitable diets and advise about health care and vaccination programmes.

How do you tell the difference between a good and bad breeder?

- Obtain basic information from the Canadian Kennel Club or the relevant breeding association.
- Get information from dog clubs in your area.
- Talk to owners of the breed you are thinking of buying, find out if they are having any problems and where they got their animals from.

TOP: If you are not sure which breed of dog is the best for your needs, talk to your vet, as she or he deals with many different dogs every day and can offer valuable advice.

- aged between seven and eight weeks
- fully weaned
- strong enough to cope on its own away from its mother
- still with its mother (to enable you to assess the temperament of the bitch)
- alert, bright and healthy
- not overly aggressive towards humans or littermates
- willing to come to you
- clean around the eyes, ears, nose and anal area, and have a healthy skin.

The breeder should:

- provide complete information on the puppy's present and future diet
- provide pedigree papers if necessary
- provide records of any worming or vaccinations.

You should:

- try to get the breeder to agree to a short approval period, in case there are problems
- take the puppy on condition that it is given a thorough veterinary check-up
- then get it checked by a vet as soon as you get it
- never obtain a puppy from a litter in which there appears to be any type of disease.

Selecting for temperament

You are likely to want a puppy with the ideal temperament described in the breed standards and norms. However, within any breed there are great variations between individuals and strains.

Selection for temperament starts with the breeder. A reputable breeder checks all the puppies for temperament and follows their progress.

Some breeders concentrate on the physical characteristics of the breed, which will win awards in the show ring; they pay less regard to breeding good temperament.

- Talk to your local veterinarian. Owners of dogs that have physical or behaviour problems as a result of poor breeding programmes usually consult vets, so these professionals get a pretty good indication of which breeders are doing the best job.

Once you have located some reputable breeders, find out why they are breeding. Some breed specifically for show, but success in the show ring does not necessarily mean that the offspring will suit you. Check out the incidence of any inherited conditions in their dogs, and if in doubt get advice about this from your vet.

Choosing the puppy

Never buy a puppy on the spur of the moment. Plan well ahead, allowing plenty of time for correct selection and preparation for the new arrival.

If possible, visit the breeder before the bitch whelps. Try to see both parents, and visit the puppies regularly during the suckling period. Make sure that you have a choice of puppy, rather than having a particular individual 'allocated' to you.

If you don't want to show your dog, you may be able to obtain a puppy on a 'pet only' basis. You pay less for it, but there are conditions attached. These usually state that it cannot be registered as a pedigree dog, it must not be bred from, and may not have pups.

TOP: When you introduce your new puppy to your 'current' dog, they'll need to establish the hierarchy between the two of them. The puppy will usually submit to the naturally dominant, older dog.

Today, however, judges at dog shows pay more attention to temperament, and fault dogs that transgress.

Always buy from a reputable breeder, and check out the temperament of the puppy's mother (and father, too, where possible). This may help to eliminate any problems in the future, but the way a puppy behaves when young will not necessarily remain the same as it gets older. The most submissive puppy in a litter may become quite bold once it is away from its littermates and established in a new home, for example.

A dog's temperament can be influenced by the temperament of its owner and the environment in which it lives, too, so you and your family will have a great deal of influence on how it behaves.

TOP: Although the Labrador Retriever is regarded as the perfect example of a canine member of a human family, individuals do not always live up to the breed's reputation of being affable, agreeable and family oriented.

CARING FOR YOUR DOG
From grooming to boarding

Whether it's a puppy or a new-to-you adult, your dog's temperament, its enjoyment of life and its health are very much influenced by the way you and your family treat it.

A home for your new puppy

Between the age of three and 16 weeks a puppy goes through a particularly important learning period. During this time, new experiences will leave a lasting impression.

When it arrives at your home your new puppy will have lost the company and comfort of its mother and littermates, and will be in a strange environment. It is important that you begin the process of socialisation, gently integrating your new pet into your family and teaching it to relate to people and other animals through interaction and having pleasant encounters with your family members, friends and pets.

Freedom from stress

Avoid sudden loud noises, such as the slamming of doors or children's screams. Initially, limit the number of people with whom the puppy comes into contact, gradually allowing it to get used to more and more strange faces.

Don't allow children to handle the puppy too much, or disturb it when it is resting or sleeping.

Comfort

Provide a warm, comfortable bed. If you can't afford a proper dog bed or basket, use a large cardboard box with the sides cut down slightly. Line the bottom with a thick layer of newspaper and top this with a washable blanket. If you decide to buy a proper dog bed or basket, make sure it is large enough to accommodate your puppy as it grows.

Place the puppy's bed where you want it to sleep as an adult – choose a quiet, private corner. For the first few nights a big cuddly toy and a warm (not hot) water bottle beneath the bedding will help the puppy to settle. The puppy may be noisy and distressed at night immediately after separation from its littermates. A low radio or ticking clock can help soothe it.

During its waking hours, give the puppy plenty of body contact. Talk to your puppy, using a soft voice to express friendship and a gruff voice to express disapproval of any of its unwanted actions.

ABOVE: This teething Dogue de Bordeaux finds some relief in his squeaky toy.

TOP: It is essential that your puppy has a quiet, private corner in which to sleep.

Safety precautions

When preparing for your new puppy's arrival, consider safety in the home, just as you would for a young child.

- Lock away household chemicals or poisons and remove car and garden toxins such as windshield washer and ant traps.
- Keep electrical cords out of biting reach.
- Don't leave medications or food wrapped in plastic, foil or paper packaging where your puppy can reach it.
- Make sure your puppy can't get into garbage cans.
- Be aware of the risks associated with some common house and garden plants, such as azaleas and crocus.
- Remember that sparks from an open fire or hot cigarette ash can damage the eyes or skin.
- Anyone using mowers, bicycles, skateboards, roller

blades and similar articles must be extra vigilant.

- Check where the puppy is before moving a car.
- Make sure that your puppy cannot get through fencing around a swimming pool.

ABOVE: The typical Basset Hound gets on well with children, and can cope in both hot and cool climates. However, it is notorious for being able to find food in any hidden spot in the home.

TOP: A selection of safe, chewable dog toys.

Food and water

Start by feeding your puppy the same diet it ate before it joined your family.

Introduce any changes over several days to avoid causing digestive upsets.

Specially formulated and fully balanced commercial puppy diets are strongly recommended. Make sure that clean, fresh water is always available. A deep, stainless-steel or earthenware bowl will keep the water cooler, and in summer ice can be added.

Play, toys and chewing

Puppies thrive on play. Among their own littermates it gives them exercise and it is how they learn to compete for their order in the pack. Don't be rough with your puppy, but in these early games it is important that the puppy learns that the family members are dominant, so express disapproval if it tries to get the upper hand.

Puppies chew objects partly because it helps them through the teething process and partly because it is a way of investigating their environment. Satisfy this need with chewable toys or objects, but make sure these are:

o   made of safe materials
o   large enough so that they cannot be swallowed
o   not similar to objects that you do not want chewed. For example, if you provide your puppy with an old slipper to chew, don't be surprised if it decides to cut its teeth on one of your expensive shoes. It will be too young to have learned the difference. Rawhide chews are ideal, because your puppy cannot mistake them for anything else.

House-training

It is best to adopt your puppy when it is seven or eight weeks old, as it is around this time that it is beginning to

Infections you could catch from your dog

Some dog infections can be passed on to humans: rabies; intestinal parasites such as roundworms, hookworms and tapeworms; leptospirosis and other bacterial infections such as campylobacter and salmonella; and ringworm infection.

o   Avoid contamination from a dog's urine or faeces.
o   Always wash your hands after handling a dog.
o   Don't allow a dog to lick your face.
o   Don't eat food that may have been licked by a dog.

House rules

Your puppy is a member of your family 'pack', which includes humans and other family pets. You must teach it that you are the pack leader, and that it is the bottom dog in the pack. Once it recognises its place in your family hierarchy it will be more contented and more easily trained to obey commands. The puppy will look to its pack leader to protect it and make decisions for it.

You will need to start teaching your new puppy house rules. Then, once it has settled in, you can start to teach it the basic commands (see pp56–9, Training your dog).

TOP: An old shoe makes a wonderful chewy toy, but can this Boxer distinguish it from your brand-new pair?
TOP CENTRE: Puppies love to play, and it is one way they learn to compete for dominance in the pack.

develop what is known as a 'substrate preference': the selection of a specific substance and area on which to eliminate. This means that it will very quickly become accustomed to using grass or soil as a toilet area if given ready access and encouraged to do so.

Anticipate toilet needs. Take your puppy outside as soon as it wakes up, as well as before and after every meal, after a period of vigorous play or exercise and whenever you see it looking distracted, walking in circles and sniffing the ground. It is very important to go right outside with the puppy, take it to a specific area of the garden and wait until it has eliminated. Always praise it afterwards. Never stand at the door and wait for the puppy to take itself outside. The chances are it will wander off a little way and then come straight back to find you – without relieving itself.

If you wish, you can use a word command (many trainers use the word 'peepee') when you take the puppy outside. It will soon learn to associate the word with the action. Once that is taught, you can train it to eliminate at home rather than in a public place. Always clean up the faeces (a poop-scoop is ideal) and dispose of them properly.

Never allow a young puppy free access to the entire house. It can easily become disorientated and relieve itself in one of the rooms. You need to be there to take it outside if it needs to go.

Young puppies have small bladders and poor bladder control. Don't expect a young puppy to manage without urinating from 8pm to 8am. Take it out late at night – 11pm is a good time, and get up at 5am to let it out once more.

If your puppy eliminates in the house, do not become angry and punish it. If you have not seen the puppy make the mistake, just clean it up and forget about it. If you catch the puppy in the act, say 'no' firmly. Then pick up the puppy, take it outside and praise it while it is on the grass. If possible, take the 'mistake' out with you on a paper towel so that the puppy associates the waste product with the out-door surface.

Because a puppy has an attention span of only a few seconds, you cannot demonstrate that something is wrong some time after it was done.

Socialisation

Your puppy will need to learn to socialise with any other animals in your household.

If you own a cat, ask your vet to trim its claws to avoid it damaging the puppy's eyes. Do not allow the puppy to chase the cat, and if necessary keep it on a lead when the cat is around. Distract it whenever it wants to chase the cat and gradually encourage closer contact in a controlled manner.

If you own another dog, introduce the dog and puppy outside the house. Give the older dog plenty of attention and supervise all play. Feed the two dogs separately, and do not leave them alone together until the puppy is well settled in. Even then, though, it is wise to provide the puppy with an area into which it can escape from the other dog. Try something such as a wooden box or a kennel with a door too small for the larger dog.

Don't allow your puppy to meet with neighbourhood dogs until it has completed its vaccination programme. If possible enrol the puppy in a puppy kindergarten (see pp56, Training your dog).

If you own other types of animals, introduce these to the puppy early on. Allow the puppy to be present when you are attending to them, and encourage the puppy to behave gently.

Allow the puppy to meet human visitors, but make sure that such meetings are carried out gently and quietly so that the puppy enjoys the experience.

ABOVE: Remember that if you house-train a puppy on newspaper, this will become its 'substrate preference', and it could relieve itself on your weekend papers. However, as many dog owners live in apartments without gardens and grass, this method of house-training is the most practical.

Prevent children who visit from handling the puppy roughly, and make sure the puppy has somewhere to which it can escape when it has had enough.

Territory

Confine your puppy to a small area of your home until it is properly toilet-trained. A mobile playpen can prove very successful indoors, and can also be used to allow the puppy some time outside in the garden.

Once it is toilet-trained, your puppy can be given as much freedom around the house as you choose.

Make sure that your garden is properly fenced and that gates have return springs and catches on them. Because dogs are naturally territorial, it won't be long before your puppy learns to recognise the boundaries of its own property.

You must limit contact with other dogs until it has completed a course of vaccinations, usually at the age of 12 or 16 weeks. You can attend a reputable puppy kindergarten (preferably run in association with a veterinary clinic) before the puppy's vaccination programme is complete, because these schools should be held in a disease-free environment (see p56, Training your dog).

Avoid parks, forests and other public places where other dog owners walk their pets.

If local laws permit, it is safe to take your puppy for early morning walks on the beach below the high-tide mark – the sand will have been washed overnight by the high tide and is unlikely to have been contaminated since.

Do not go onto the dry sand, though, and do not allow the puppy to have any contact with other dogs that might arrive while you are there. And, of course, you will need to clean up after your puppy, for the sake of other walkers.

Vaccinations

See p81, Protecting your dog's health.

Worming

See pp85-90, Protecting your dog's health.

Flea control

See pp91-92, Protecting your dog's health.

Leash training and exercise

Once it is fully vaccinated, your puppy will benefit from regular exercise, and by then you will need to have trained it to wear a collar and walk on a leash.

Collar and leash training

See pp61–2, Training your dog.

Exercising your puppy

Exercise your puppy only to a degree that it can comfortably manage. Don't force it, and don't attach it to a bike or person in such a way that it has to exercise regardless of how it feels. A retractable leash is ideal, as it gives the puppy a

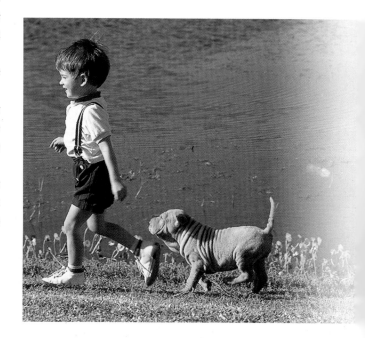

ABOVE: When puppies are able to exercise with children, it is easier for them to pace themselves and not overdo it.
TOP LEFT: A dog with fresh breath? A proper diet and early 'toothbrush training' will take care of dental hygiene.
TOP RIGHT: A grooming mitt should be part of your basic grooming equipment.

chance to pace itself. Stop exercise immediately if it begins to look tired or stressed.

If you want to run with your puppy, limit this activity to very short spells. Be very careful with a puppy of a large breed, because its bone growth is much slower than average and excessive exercise can cause ligament or bone damage. If in doubt, don't run with it, and talk to your vet or breeder.

Before going out, use your chosen word command to try to get it to eliminate at home (see p32, House-training). If this is not successful and it eliminates while you are out, make sure you pick up the droppings and dispose of them properly – many local authorities now provide dog waste containers. Dog faeces containing certain roundworm or hookworm eggs or larvae can be a hazard to human health (see pp85-90, Protecting your dog's health).

Teething

Between the ages of three and six months your puppy's temporary (milk) teeth will gradually be shed and replaced by permanent teeth. The timing varies between breeds and individuals, but shedding usually starts with the incisors, followed by the premolar, molar and canine teeth.

You can help your puppy through this teething process by providing a mixture of soft foods and hard, chewable foods such as dog biscuits. Rawhide chews are ideal for young puppies. The chewing action helps to loosen the temporary teeth, and is also beneficial for tartar control.

Dental hygiene

For dogs, as with humans, a proper diet will help to keep teeth clean and gums healthy. Nevertheless, tartar may begin to accumulate on the teeth, especially as a dog gets older, and they should be checked regularly.

Dog toothpaste is available from vets. Train your puppy so that it will allow you to apply this with a soft toothbrush.

Special diets are available that will clean teeth through their mildly abrasive action. Talk to your vet about these.

Grooming your dog
Brushing and combing

As soon as you get your puppy you should get it used to being groomed, handled and examined. Establish a daily routine in which the puppy is gently placed onto a non-slip surface (a piece of old carpet or something similar), either on the floor or on a table, and rolled over to have its mouth, teeth, eyes, ears, abdomen, paws and other parts of its anatomy examined. Although it may not need grooming, do it anyway. This routine will train your puppy to accept being handled and groomed, and you will more quickly detect fleas or flea dirt, and any hair or skin problems.

Try to make each session pleasant for the puppy, and praise and reward it for good behaviour.

Your basic grooming equipment should include a dog brush, comb, grooming glove (mitt), sponge, cotton wool balls, dog towel, blunt-ended surgical scissors and nail clippers.

Dog brushes are especially designed for different types of coat. Those with soft bristles will avoid damage to the sensitive skin of fine-coated breeds.

Brushes with hard bristles can be used on thick-coated breeds. Rubber brushes can be used for breeds with very short, close coats (Boxers, for example), whereas soft, pin brushes are ideal for breeds with long, fine coats such as the Yorkshire Terrier.

TOP LEFT: A hard bristle brush is ideal for thick-coated dogs.
ABOVE RIGHT: A double-sided comb and an undercoat rake.

Combs also vary. Those with wide teeth are used on long, fine coats, while those with narrow teeth are suitable for other types of coat and can be used to remove tangles from the ears, leg feathers or tail. There is also a special comb, called an undercoat rake, which makes the removal of thick undercoat easier. It is particularly useful for breeds such as Labrador Retrievers and German Shepherd Dogs (Alsatians).

You will spend more time grooming a long-coated breed than a short-coated one. Pay special attention to the feathering on the legs, and the tail. Also check the paws, nails and paw pads. Use a wet sponge to wash away any mud that has accumulated on the hair between the pads, to prevent it building up and causing inflammation. As your puppy gets bigger, hair may grow beyond the level of the pads. If so, trim it away using a pair of blunt-ended, curved surgical scissors.

Use a damp cotton wool ball to wipe away 'sleep' from your dog's eyes. Check under the tail, wipe away any debris and cut away any excess hair that might lead to soiling.

Bathing

If you carry out regular grooming, you should need to bath your dog only if it gets very dirty or smelly.

Always give your dog a thorough brush-out before bathing it. Use lukewarm water (which is more comfortable, especially for a puppy) and a proper dog shampoo. Place a cotton wool ball in each ear to prevent water from entering, and don't let shampoo get into any body opening. Rinse off thoroughly, paying special attention to the areas between the forelegs and hind legs.

A puppy can easily become chilled, so make sure you dry it properly, using its own special towel. If you prefer to use a hair drier, run your fingers through the dog's hair as it is being dried to make sure that the air stream is not too hot.

Nails

Dogs' nails, like those of humans, are continually growing. Puppies need their nails clipped about every six weeks, with special dog nail clippers. It is possible to do them yourself, but perhaps rather ask a vet or dog groomer.

Many adult dogs spend little time walking on hard surfaces, so their nails don't wear down naturally. Nail growth and wear varies according to breed and conditions, so clip them as necessary.

If your puppy has dew claws, regularly check their length. Unless properly trimmed, the claws may catch in objects and get torn. In extreme cases the nails may eventually curl round and grow back into the skin.

Dog groomers and grooming parlours

Many breeds require a considerable amount of grooming. Other breeds require clipping if their owner wants them to conform to the breed's usual appearance or enter them into shows. If you are sure that you know exactly what to do, and if you have the time, you can do all this grooming yourself. If not, get an expert to do it for you. If you would like to learn to groom your dog, ask at your nearest grooming parlour or vet for details of grooming schools and courses.

ABOVE: As most dogs spend their time on soft outdoor terrain or carpets, their nails don't wear down naturally. You'll need to clip their nails regularly – if you're unsure, ask your vet to do so.

Neutering

Unless your dog is to be used for pedigree breeding, have it neutered, or in the case of a female, spayed. Ideally, females should be spayed at five to six months, before their first oestrus period. Males should be neutered at about six months. Ask your veterinarian for advice.

As well as averting unwanted pregnancies or adding to the number of puppies in need of good homes, these procedures help reduce the risk of prostate cancer in male dogs and mammary cancer in bitches. Neutering also reduces a male dog's sex drive, and therefore its levels of frustration.

Day care

If you regularly have to leave your dog alone for more than four hours at a stretch, consider employing a dog walker or dog sitter. A full, eight-hour working day is too long to regularly leave it alone; dogs left for long periods are more likely to develop bad habits or anti-social behaviour. And, while another dog may provide company, cat companionship is unlikely to be enough for a dog – although it would help.

Travelling with your dog

The law

Whenever you take your dog away from home, put your name and telephone number on a dog tag fastened to its collar. If your dog gets lost, you have a better chance of being re-united.

Ensure you know the animal bylaws that apply locally. Most municipalities require that dogs be licensed, vaccinated against diseases such as rabies and distemper, and kept on a leash in public places. Some cities ban breeds such as Pit Bulls, and require owners to carry liability insurance for certain aggressive breeds. Dogs may be prohibited altogether in parks and on beaches, or restricted to certain seasons or times of day. In most places you are expected to clean up after your dog and remove the waste.

In your car

If possible, train your dog from puppyhood so that it becomes used to travelling. This will help eliminate any fear or agitation, and reduce the likelihood of motion sickness.

Do not allow your dog to have complete freedom within a vehicle. It can distract the driver and lead to an accident, and the dog is at risk of injury if an accident occurs. For its own safety a dog should ride in the rear of a station wagon or hatchback. Fit a special grill or dog guard to prevent it from jumping onto the seats in front.

If your dog has to travel on the back seat, fasten it into a seat belt. If it is small enough, train it to ride comfortably in a plastic travelling container that is fastened to a seat belt or placed where it will not move if you brake suddenly.

If there is room to put a dog crate in your vehicle, train your dog to ride in one. It eventually becomes an extension of its home territory, and your dog will feel comfortable inside and readily occupy it. Crates are commonly used by people who show their dogs, and are an ideal way of providing a safe, secure, 'personal space' for your canine companion. Once your dog is accustomed to it, the crate can accompany it wherever it goes, providing it with a 'home away from home'.

TOP: Although a dog and cat living in the same household may become very tolerant of and even affectionate with each other, felines are generally too aloof and independent to act as reliable day-care companions for a lonely dog.

If you have to leave your dog in your car, do so only briefly, make sure that the vehicle is parked in the shade and has adequate ventilation. In the sun, the temperature inside a closed car can exceed 40° C (104° F), and heatstroke will set in very rapidly. Even with window ventilation, a parked car becomes unbearably hot in high temperatures. Do not assume that a car parked in the shade will remain so: as the sun moves around, a shady area may become fully exposed. Special screens can be fixed to open windows to prevent escape.

On holiday

Make sure that your dog's vaccinations are up to date, as the incidence of infectious disease in your holiday area may be greater than in your home neighbourhood. Different sorts of external parasite, such as ticks, may also be present, so thoroughly groom your dog every day and check its skin for their presence.

In a bus, train or plane

If you are taking some form of commercial transport, check with the carrier. Your dog may be required to travel separately in a crate. This can be frightening for a dog that has not been crate-trained, so train it to feel safe in its own crate, with its own familiar toys and bedding.

Don't feed your dog six hours before the start of the journey. If you think your dog may suffer from motion sickness, ask your vet for advice. Be sure to carry out all training procedures recommended by your carrier.

Travelling between countries

Travel between countries usually involves travel documentation for you and your dog. Regulations vary, so make sure you know what they are for the particular country you are heading for. You will probably need a veterinary certificate stating that your dog is fit to travel and is free from any infectious or contagious disease. You will also need an up-to-date rabies vaccination certificate. Many countries require these documents to be in their own language.

There are many places where rabies does not exist, such as Greece, Italy, Portugal, Spain, Sweden, Norway, Switzerland, England, Scotland, Wales, Ireland and Northern Ireland. Some countries require a dog to be quarantined upon entry, while others will allow entry providing that certain conditions, such as microchip identification and blood testing, have been met (see PETS below). Contact the consulate or embassy of the country concerned.

PET Travel Scheme (PETS)

Canadian pet lovers have watched with interest a pilot scheme for the issue of 'pet passports', which was introduced in Britain in 2000. Under this scheme, dogs and cats may travel from the British Isles to specified countries in western Europe without being quarantined upon their return. Owners must use designated carriers and ports of entry. Under the same scheme dogs and cats from specified European countries are allowed to enter the British Isles.

TOP: Your dog is unlikely to enjoy travelling in a cage, Nevertheless, you can make the experience less traumatic by gradually introducing your dog to the idea ahead of time.

Dogs resident in the British Isles: To qualify for a 'pet passport' a dog resident in the British Isles must have an identification microchip inserted under the skin, and then be vaccinated against rabies by an approved veterinarian. Some time after the last vaccine injection (30 days is the ideal period), a blood sample needs to be taken by the veterinarian and sent to one of the government-approved laboratories. Once the blood sample passes the test, a health certificate or passport is issued and stamped by the veterinarian.

Between 24 and 48 hours before returning to Britain, the animal must be treated against a particular tapeworm (*Echinococcus multilocularis*) and ticks, and a health certificate must be issued by a veterinarian approved by the relevant government.

Once vaccinated against rabies, annual booster shots will keep your dog rabies free and his passport up to date.

Dogs resident in Europe: Animals resident in specified countries in Europe can also qualify to enter Britain if their owners follow the same rules. However, their owners must wait for six months from the time a successful blood test sample was taken.

Dogs resident in rabies-free islands: Providing that the relevant veterinary authorities and the airline carriers agree, dogs and cats may be allowed to travel between Britain and designated islands that are rabies-free. These include Australia, Hawaii, Japan, New Zealand, Singapore and Taiwan.

Dogs resident in Canada and the United States: Because rabies is endemic in North America, the original PET Travel Scheme did not apply to dogs entering from Canada and the United States. At present, these dogs must still endure a six-month quarantine period in Britain. The situation will be reviewed once the success of the initial scheme has been assessed.

Boarding

Early training at being parted from you can help your dog to cope. You could leave it with a relative, friend or neighbour for short periods to get it used to being separated, and to learn that you will be coming back.

The standard of boarding kennels varies. Usually (but not always) you get what you pay for, so the more expensive the fees the better the quality of comfort and service you should expect.

A reputable kennel will allow you to inspect its facilities beforehand. If you do so, observe how the resident dogs are behaving and talk to the staff about feeding, grooming and exercise routines. The staff at your local veterinary hospital may be able to recommend a suitable boarding kennel, and will advise on vaccination procedures.

Dog sitters

If you don't like the idea of boarding your dog, you may wish to employ the services of a dog-sitter or house sitter to provide live-in care of your home and dog during your absence. Check with your vet to find out which ones are approved in your locality.

ABOVE: If you plan to take your dog with you when you emigrate, bear in mind that it may have to be kept in quarantine for up to six months in certain countries. Finding another owner might be a kinder option, as your pet will not understand the situation and will suffer from separation anxiety and loneliness.

NUTRITION
A balanced diet

The wolf and other wild members of the dog family (*Canidae*) are carnivores and eat a great deal of animal protein. But because a diet of meat alone does not contain many essential nutrients, they consume a variety of vegetable matter, either directly or in the stomach contents of their prey, as well as other types of food, including insects.

Nutrients and a balanced diet

Dogs, like wolves, cannot remain healthy on a diet of meat alone. They also need fat, carbohydrates, minerals, vitamins and fibre. (If you wish to incorporate large amounts of vegetable protein in your dog's diet, consult your veterinarian.)

Energy

Dogs must be fed enough calories (KCal) to satisfy their energy needs, which vary according to their age, size and the amount of exercise or work they perform. The amount of energy that a dog requires is also related to the surface area of its body, because this influences how much heat it loses. On a kilo-per-kilo, pound-per-pound basis, a small dog has a comparatively larger surface area than a large dog. A dog weighing 2.5kg/5.5lb has 300% more surface area per kilogram of body weight than a dog weighing 50kg/110lb, so the smaller one needs more energy kilo per kilo, pound per pound.

To determine the exact amount your dog needs, monitor its weight and health. Overweight dogs, like overweight humans, are more likely to have health problems.

When very high intakes of energy or nutrients are needed, such as when a dog is performing hard work (racing or sled pulling) or a bitch is in late pregnancy, they must be in sufficiently concentrated form to enable the dog to physically eat the quantity of food required. Properly formulated commercial diets will ensure this.

Comparative energy requirements

100%	Sedentary
400%	Bitch during late pregnancy/lactation
300%	Very hard work
200%	Moderate work
170%	Very cold weather
150%	Slight stress (eg showing or training)

Giant breeds could need up to 50% more energy than shown in the table, and there may be a variation of 20% either way, depending on the dog.

Diets for different situations

Dogs need different types of diet according to:
- age or stage of growth – puppy, juvenile, adult or elderly
- the amount of exercise/work they perform

TOP: The lower molars and the upper pre-molars of the mostly carnivorous wolf are specially adapted for cutting and tearing meat.

- breed – large breeds mature later than small breeds, and giant breeds have special needs
- size – there can be significant differences in size within a breed
- their state of health
- whether a bitch is pregnant or lactating.

Suggested levels of nutrients for dogs

Note: These figures are expressed as a percentage of dry matter in the diet.

	Protein	Suggested Range	Fat	Carbo-hydrate
Growth	32	28–32	15	40
Adult maintenance	22	22–25	8	50
Adult hard work	34	30–36	20	34
Adult very hard work	38	36–45	25	25
Pregnancy/lactation	32	25–32	15	40
Old age	22	15–22	8	50

Recommendations vary, and these figures are given as a guide only. If you want to formulate a home-cooked diet for your dog, you should discuss it with your veterinarian.

Commercial or home-cooked foods?

If you choose home-cooked foods, you need to consider the considerable time involved in preparation. Will you always be able to manage to keep up with a home-cooked diet? And can you accurately provide all the nutritional requirements for your dog?

You may also need to consider value for money. Most owners base their dog's diet on commercial foods, but may feed them a home-cooked meal from time to time. It doesn't hurt to ring the changes.

If you own a young puppy or a pregnant bitch, it is probably more sensible to choose a commercial diet, designed to provide all the nutritional requirements for growth and development. Of particular concern are calcium and phosphorus levels and their ratio (they should be equal) – it is

TOP: It is usually best to feed a young puppy a high-quality commercial diet, which has been formulated to accurately provide all the nutritional requirements.

difficult to get the balance right in a home kitchen. Geriatric dogs also need special care, and commercial diets are available to cater for their changing needs.

Commercial diets

Reputable commercial foods are based on sound research into the requirements of animals at each stage of development. Many commercial companies employ nutritional scientists and veterinarians to analyse their products and carry out controlled feeding trials to ensure that they meet international standards. The fully balanced commercial diets are easy to feed, and quantities can be accurately measured.

Commercial diets can be grouped according to moisture content (there is some variation between similar products):

○ Canned or moist foods. These have a moisture content of around 78 per cent (roughly the same as fresh meat). They do not need preservatives because cooking destroys all bacteria and the canning prevents any further contamination.

○ Dog sausages or dog rolls. These have a moisture content of around 50 per cent. They usually contain preservatives, but also require refrigeration.

○ Semi-moist foods. These have a moisture content of around 25 per cent. These foods usually contain preservatives and do not require refrigeration. They often have a high carbohydrate or sugar content, so they should not be fed to diabetic dogs.

○ Dry foods (complete diets). These have a moisture content of around 10 per cent, usually contain preservatives and do not require refrigeration. They are easily stored, hygienic and available for all breeds

and ages of dog. (There are brands free of preservatives.)

○ Biscuits. These have a moisture content of around 8 per cent. They usually contain preservatives and do not require refrigeration.

Nutritionally, there is no difference between dry foods and moist foods, as long as they contain the same amount and proportion of nutrients. In general, though, moist dog foods are more costly to the consumer because they contain water, which provides no nutrition and for which the customer pays.

There are few warning signs for an inferior product, except that the label may give little or no nutritional information. Depending on the country in which they are manufactured and/or sold, reputable foods have labels that give adequate nutritional information, and which contain a statement such as 'complete and balanced'.

The label usually lists the main food ingredients, plus an analysis of certain nutrients (protein, fat and salt) and the fibre content. Many manufacturers state the amount that should be fed relative to body weight, stage of growth and activity level. They also list the calorific value of the food (in KCal per kilogram or ounce), which may help you to determine the right amount to feed your particular dog.

Dog treats and dog chews

These usually contain high levels of fat and carbohydrate. Offer them to your dog when it needs something to keep it interested, or as a reward. Do make allowances for their high energy content, though, and reduce your dog's normal food intake accordingly.

There is no nutritional difference between moist foods and dry foods (TOP LEFT AND RIGHT), although moist foods are usually more expensive. Serve high-fat dog treats (ABOVE LEFT AND RIGHT) as rewards and modify your dog's normal food intake accordingly.

Foods from the veterinary clinic

Some commercial dog foods are sold through veterinary clinics and/or pet stores only. Referred to as professional formulae, they differ from supermarket foods in that their constituents are guaranteed. They do not contain the textured vegetable protein (TVP) found in some supermarket pet foods.

Other foods sold only through veterinary clinics are therapeutic diets formulated to assist in the management of health problems. Special diets are available for pregnant or lactating bitches, to assist dogs convalescing after surgery or trauma, or for those undergoing treatment for anaemia or cancer.

There are also diets designed to help with oral hygiene, and biscuits that help reduce plaque build-up.

Home-cooked diets

If you intend to feed mainly a home-cooked diet, make sure that the mixture of foods will supply the right types and quantities of nutrients.

WARNING

Excessive supplementation with vitamins and minerals can cause serious health problems.

A popular type of home-cooked meal is lean mince or cheap meat cuts cooked together in a pressure cooker with a mixture of vegetables and perhaps pasta or rice. You can prepare this meal in bulk and freeze dinner-size packs. A commercial dog biscuit may be fed for breakfast, and the main meat meal fed at night.

Cooking food destroys some vitamins, and overcooking can greatly reduce a food's nutritional value. You would therefore need to supplement cooked foods with the right types and amounts of vitamins, just as reputable pet food manufacturers do.

Supplements usually contain calcium carbonate or bone meal (to create the right balance of phosphorus and calcium), iodine, vitamin A and vitamin D. Properly formulated supplements and herbal preparations are available from pet stores and/or veterinarians. Before using any you should talk to your veterinarian.

Supplementation may be necessary under certain conditions, such as stress or illness – ask your veterinarian for advice; special therapeutic diets are also available.

A home-made maintenance diet

This diet is for maintenance only – when a dog is already in good health and not under any stress. It is formulated to balance the nutritional deficiencies in meat. Liver provides vitamins A, D and E and various B vitamins. Corn oil provides essential fatty acids, while bone meal provides calcium and phosphorus in the correct proportions. Iodised salt provides iodine.

This quantity is for a 10kg (22lb) dog, and should be adjusted for dogs that are lighter or heavier. The serving size

Rice, brown or white (dry)	140g (5oz)
Meat (medium fat)	70g (2.5oz)
Liver	30g (1oz)
Bone meal	8g (.3oz)
Iodised salt	3g (.1oz)
Corn oil	5ml (one teaspoon)
Water	420ml (14 fl oz)

TOP: The ingredients for a home-made maintenance diet: make sure that the mixture provides the correct types and quantities of nutrients.

will depend on the calorie requirements of the dog – the total energy value of this quantity formula is 750 KCal. This formula will keep in the refrigerator for a few days. However, like us, dogs enjoy freshly cooked food, which tastes better than 'cold warmed up' meals.

Mix the rice and water and simmer for about 20 minutes. Add the other ingredients and simmer for a further 10 minutes.

A meatier, more tasty diet can be prepared by transposing the quantities of rice and meat. The energy value will be the same, but the diet will contain almost twice the protein.

Ingredients for home-cooked meals

Even if you intend to serve only commercially prepared foods to your dog, don't skip this section. It contains useful information about serving those little extras: eggs, milk and oils, for example.

Meat and meat by-products: All forms of red or white meat provide protein, B-group vitamins, fat and energy, but the relative amounts depend on the type of meat and also on the cut.

	Protein (average %)	Fat (average %)	Energy (KlCal/100g/3.5 oz)
Beef	20	4.5	122
Chicken	20	4.5	122
Lamb	20	8.8	162

All meat is seriously deficient in calcium and slightly deficient in phosphorus, and the proportion of phosphorus to calcium is greatly excessive, ranging from about 10:1 for rabbit and beef heart to 30:1 for veal and 360:1 for fresh liver. Dogs need a 1:1.3 phosphorus to calcium ratio.

Meat is also deficient in vitamins A and D and iodine, copper, iron, magnesium and sodium. Cheap cuts will be as

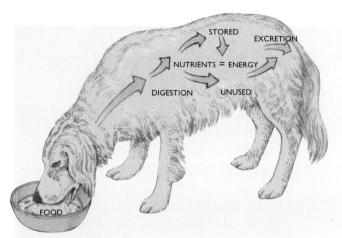

The 'food-chain': the process of digestion in a dog

nutritious as expensive ones, but whichever you buy should be cooked. (In an effort to eliminate the hydatid tapeworm [see p89], certain countries require that all sheep or goat meat must either be cooked to a certain temperature or deep frozen at a given temperature for a minimum period of time.)

Cooking destroys much of meat's vitamin B content.

Liver is a valuable food rich in protein, fat, the fat-soluble vitamins A, D and E and the B vitamins. Too much vitamin A can lead to abnormal bone growth, but cooking reduces the liver's vitamin A content. As a general guide, do not let liver form more than 15 per cent of your dog's diet.

Chicken is considered to be more digestible than red meat, while some dogs are allergic to certain proteins contained in red meat and may develop a skin irritation.

Fish: There are two main types of fish: white, which has a nutrient composition similar to lean meat; and fatty or oily, which contains high levels of vitamins A and D. All fish contains high-quality protein and iodine, but is deficient in calcium, phosphorus, copper, iron, magnesium and sodium.

Take care not to feed your dog raw (filleted) fish, as it contains thiaminase, an enzyme that destroys

THIS PAGE AND OPPOSITE: Those little extras beloved by dogs: even if you serve your dogs a commercially prepared diet, eggs, cheese, fish, fats and vegetables can offer highly nutritious variations.

thiamine, one of the B vitamins. Never give fish heads or fish offal. Cook any fish you serve. Oily fish (such as tuna) contains high levels of unsaturated fatty acids, and too much may cause a painful inflammation of fat deposits under the skin (steatitis).

Fish bones should be fed only if previously softened by pressure cooking or grinding in a blender. Boiling or stewing would also soften the bones, but the longer cooking time would destroy more of the nutrients. Whole fish cooked in a pressure cooker is nutritionally better than meat, as it has a better balance of nutrients.

Eggs: Eggs contain iron, protein, most vitamins (except for vitamin C) and carbohydrates, and are particularly good if fed raw. However, too much raw egg may be harmful, as egg white contains a substance called avidin that can reduce the availability of the B vitamin biotin (essential for many body processes, including health of skin and hair and proper muscle function). As a guide, feed no more than two raw eggs per week to a 30kg (66lb) dog. If you feed the egg yolk only, you may increase the number of eggs to four. Hard boiling reduces the avidin, although this slightly reduces the nutritional value of the eggs.

Milk and cheese: Dairy produce is high in protein, fat, carbohydrate, calcium, phosphorus and vitamin A and the B vitamins.

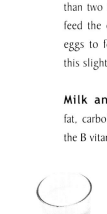

Milk is a useful source of calcium for puppies, although not all dogs will drink it. It contains milk sugar (lactose), and as puppies mature their ability to digest this decreases – if fed more than small quantities of milk they may develop diarrhoea. Some adult dogs are lactose intolerant, and if fed milk they will develop an allergic, dry, itchy skin condition. Cheese is a useful source of animal protein, and most dogs like it. Serve it in chunks. It contains little or no lactose, so it can be fed to dogs that are known to have an intolerance.

Fats and oils: Fat acts as a carrier for fat-soluble vitamins (A, D, E and K), and contains substances called fatty acids (one of which is linoleic acid) that promote a healthy skin and coat; a deficiency produces an itchy skin that may become dry and scaly.

Fat is almost 100 per cent digestible and adds palatability to food. Vegetable oils and fish fats are nutritionally better than animal fats. If the diet is not already balanced, you can feed very small amounts of cod liver oil (5ml/1 teaspoon per 50kg/110lb of body weight, or 20 small drops per 10kg/22lb of body weight, per day). Excessive amounts may cause a painful inflammation of fat under the skin, called steatitis.

Never feed your dog used cooking oil, for it may contain toxic substances called peroxides.

Vegetables: Dogs, like cats, can synthesise vitamin C in their body and don't require a dietary source.

Vegetables are a good source of B-group vitamins, but overcooking will destroy these. So, just as with cooking for humans, it is best to lightly cook in a little water. The cooking water can be added to the meal as well. Root vegetables are a good source of vitamin A, and should be cooked to increase digestibility.

Peas and beans provide protein, energy and B vitamins, and soya beans are a particularly rich source of protein and energy. One drawback to feeding peas and beans is their tendency to form gas during digestion and cause flatulence. Flatulence can also result from feeding high levels of milk or milk products, high protein diets, potatoes, cauliflower, cabbage and onions, to name but a few!

Grains: Grains provide carbohydrate, and some proteins, minerals and vitamins. They are generally deficient in fat, essential fatty acids and the fat-soluble vitamins A, D and E. Wheat germ contains thiamine and vitamin E.

Yeast: Rich in B vitamins and some minerals, yeast preparations may be good for older dogs and are safe even in excess.

Fibre: Your dog's normal diet should contain about five per cent fibre (measured on a dry basis), derived from vegetable matter. Fibre-rich diets (10–15 per cent) may be used to help reduce obesity, and can also be used as a dietary aid in diabetic dogs, because fibre slows the absorption of glucose (the end-product of carbohydrate digestion).

Bones: These contain 30 per cent calcium and 15 per cent phosphorus, magnesium and some proteins. They are deficient in fat and essential fatty acids and vitamins. Bone meal has a similar nutrient content. Too much bone in the diet will cause hard white faeces and may lead to constipation.

Never feed chicken or chop bones, as they will splinter, and feed fish bones only if they have been pressure-cooked.

Water: Make sure that clean, fresh water is always available. A dog's normal daily requirement (from feeding and drinking) is about 40ml (1.4 fl oz) per kg (2.2lb) of body weight. Water intake will vary according to the temperature and your dog's diet, increasing in proportion to the amount of dry food it consumes. It also increases if a dog is suffering from ailments such as diarrhoea, diabetes or kidney disease.

Feeding your dog

Select a feeding area that can be easily cleaned, and use it routinely. Use proper, easy-to-clean dog-food bowls made of stainless steel,

ABOVE AND OPPOSITE: Growing, healthy puppies will enthusiastically consume their food and usually curl up and fall sleep soon afterwards.

earthenware or plastic, and wash them after each use. Serve the food at room temperature.

Uneaten canned food should be disposed of immediately, but semi-moist food can be left in the bowl for several hours. Dry foods can be left out all day.

Feeding your puppy: A bitch's milk is rich in protein and fat, and during the first few weeks after weaning a puppy's diet needs to reflect this. A growing puppy requires up to three times more energy intake per kg (2.2lb) of body weight than does an adult, and because it has a limited stomach capacity it must be fed several times a day on a high-energy diet.

There are many commercial brands of specially formulated puppy foods, both grain-based and meat-based, which you should consider rather than trying to formulate your own. When a puppy is young you can also feed it milk.

As a general guide, a puppy aged eight to 12 weeks should receive four meals a day of a commercial food or a home-cooked diet. You need to decide which you are going to use, and stick to it. Mixing home-cooked and commercial diets can lead to imbalances.

From three to six months feed three meals a day. If milk appears to cause diarrhoea as your puppy gets older, it could be because of the lactose in the milk.

From six to 12 months feed two meals a day. If you want to change the diet, introduce the new diet gradually: Day One – 25 per cent of new diet; Day Two – 50 per cent; Day Three – 75 per cent; Day Four – 100 per cent.

Feeding your adult dog: Most adult dogs are in the non-working, non-pregnant category, and live in temperate conditions. They can usually eat their daily ration in one meal, which satisfies their appetite better and often fits in well with a household routine.

Most owners feed their dogs in the late afternoon or early evening, and after exercise. Most dogs need to urinate and defecate within an hour or two of feeding, so late-night feeding can cause problems. You can feed your dog more often to fit in with family meal times, provided that its food intake is monitored.

Large, deep-chested breeds (such as Great Danes and Irish Wolfhounds) may develop excessive gas in the stomach if fed their whole meal at once; rather divide their daily ration.

If you are feeding two dogs, feed them separately and some distance apart, so a dominant dog cannot eat another's food.

WARNING

Do not over-feed your puppy. If growth rate and weight gain are too rapid, this may lead to conditions such as hip dysplasia. Be particularly careful if your puppy is one of the giant breeds whose growth rate is comparatively slow, for there is evidence that heavy feeding and supplementation may contribute to a shorter life span.

How much to feed: Your dog should be fed enough food to satisfy its energy needs, but no more, otherwise it will put on excess weight. The amount of energy it uses will depend not only on its activity but also on its metabolic rate. Dogs' energy needs do not increase proportionately with their body weight: the larger the dog, the less energy per kilogram of bodyweight it needs. For example, a Chihuahua weighing 2kg/4.4lb needs about 230 KCal a day, whereas a Labrador Retriever weighing 30kg/66lb (15 times the weight) needs about 1,700 KCal (just over seven times the amount of energy).

If your dog is in good condition, alert and active with a healthy skin and coat, and maintaining its proper weight, it is almost certainly getting an adequate diet. If it has a scaly skin, is shedding its coat excessively, is over- or underweight, appears dull or listless, is excessively hungry or often disinterested in food, talk to your vet. You can also tell if your dog is overweight by feeling the fat layers over the ribs and spine.

Don't feed your dog household scraps between meals. Save them to become part of its normal meal, or use them as a reward. Remember that these, and treats such as chocolate drops, contain calories and you must make allowances for them in your dog's overall diet.

Nutritional problems

These should not arise if you are feeding a properly formulated commercial diet. They may arise because a dog is:

- eating the wrong diet
- eating, but a disease is reducing its ability to absorb or use food
- not eating (anorexia) for a variety of reasons.

Underfeeding results in lack of energy, weight loss and finally starvation. It could also result in a deficiency of essential nutrients. Overfeeding causes obesity with its accompanying health problems.

Danger: poison

Safety around the home is just as important for pets as it is ·for children. Many of the plants in our gardens, as well as the substances we commonly use in the house, garden, garage or shed, can be poisonous to dogs. Puppies are particularly at risk during the stage where they chew at things, and are more likely to sample any liquid leaking from a container.

All potentially poisonous substances should be locked away, or stored safely out of a dog's reach and where a cat or other animal cannot knock them off. Substances that can give off harmful vapours should be used and stored where there is adequate ventilation.

Symptoms of poisoning

Consider the possibility of poisoning if your dog is:

- suddenly vomiting and/or has severe diarrhoea (more than two or three times within an hour)
- drooling or foaming at the mouth
- panting very heavily
- crying
- suffering intense abdominal pain
- showing signs of shock
- depressed
- trembling, uncoordinated, staggering or convulsing
- collapsed or in a coma
- showing signs of an allergic reaction, such as swelling around the face or a red rash (hives) on the belly.

What to do

- Time is critical.
- Try to identify the poison.
- Carry out the recommended emergency treatment described opposite.

TOP: A healthy, correctly fed dog will have a shiny coat and be alert, active and energetic – quite the envy of most weary, exhausted and stressed owners.

- Contact your veterinarian immediately and take your dog into the clinic.
- If you have found the dog with a poisonous or unidentified substance, take the container or package with you. The label should contain information about the antidote and treatment for that particular type of poisoning.
- If your dog has vomited, collect a specimen of the vomit in a clean container and take that with you.

Emergency treatment

If the poison is corrosive (strong acid or alkali), or if you are not sure what caused the problem:

- Do not induce vomiting.
- If the dog is conscious, flush the mouth and muzzle with large quantities of water, then give one tablespoon of egg white or olive oil.
- Take the dog to your vet immediately.

If the substance is non-corrosive, or happens to be a neurotoxin (such as snailbait):

- If the dog is conscious and has not vomited already, induce vomiting.
- Put the vomit material into a clean container.
- Take the dog and vomit material to the vet immediately.

To induce vomiting, give one of the following:

- One or two large tablespoonsful of ipecac straight down the throat.
- One heaped teaspoon of table salt in warm water.
- One tablespoon of mustard powder in a cup of warm water. Repeat every 10 minutes until the dog vomits.

Emergency antidotes

Absorbants (that absorb toxic substances): activated charcoal, up to six tablets as per package instructions, or two to three tablespoons of powder mixed in a cup of warm water.

Protectants (help to cover the stomach lining): One tablespoon of egg white or olive oil.

Against acids: One teaspoon of bicarbonate of soda.

Against alkalis: Several teaspoons of vinegar or lemon juice.

UNDERSTANDING YOUR DOG'S BEHAVIOUR
The canine social system

Although dogs can live in harmony with people and have a similar social structure, their perception of the environment is very different. As a result, they interact with their environment in a very different way. If you can understand how your dog perceives its environment, you will better understand why it behaves the way it does.

The canine social system

It is generally accepted that the behaviour of the domestic dog is derived from that of the wolf. Wolves live in groups, which often consist of a breeding pair and their offspring.

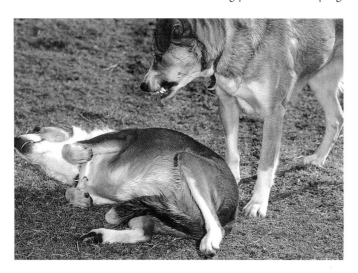

The 'alpha' (dominant) pair asserts its dominance with dominance displays: for example, staring directly at another individual, growling or standing erect with tail up and hackles raised. The subordinate or lower-ranking wolves avoid conflict by replying with submissive behaviour, such as rolling onto the side, exposing vulnerable body parts and sometimes passing urine at the same time. Usually there is one obvious hierarchy in the females and another in the males – the alpha male always partners the alpha female.

These hierarchies are 'pyramidal' – the rank differences are most obvious between high-ranking individuals but are less distinct lower down the scale.

The alpha female is highly aggressive to other females, especially around the breeding season. The alpha male is highly aggressive towards intruders, but not so aggressive to the rest of the pack; his status is accepted and the hierarchy is maintained by deference.

A human observer may quite clearly distinguish the 'beta', or second in rank, male – he is often the most aggressive animal in the pack. Mostly, his aggression is directed towards the alpha male – when the latter animal becomes older and more vulnerable, the beta male will take over.

Wolves hunt in cooperation, but dominant animals eat before subordinates.

ABOVE AND TOP: Just like wolves, dogs that are lower in the social hierarchy display submissive behaviour by tucking in their tails, rolling onto their sides or exposing vulnerable body parts.

The cubs of the alpha pair are communally raised. The other pairs don't breed, and the entire pack will care for the offspring. This vastly increases their chances of survival.

Domestic dogs vary to differing extents from this pattern. Groups of dogs do form hierarchies, although the visual expression of dominance is sometimes less evident. This may be because many modern breeds have facial and body characteristics that cannot change enough to communicate – think of breeds with short faces and stubby tails; it is difficult for them to posture in a typical canine fashion.

Modern dogs are more vocal than wolves, probably as a result of human selection of animals that would warn of intruders by barking, and also the selection of 'puppy type' characteristics (see p13).

The dog-human relationship

Dogs and humans can form close associations and bonds, probably due to similarities in their social structure. Human social systems involve leaders and followers, and this order is maintained largely by deference on the part of weaker or lower-ranking individuals to those who are more powerful or skilled. The same is true of canine society.

Dogs living with humans tend to regard them as members of a pack, and soon recognise dominance and subordination in people. Consequently, it is important to make sure that your dog is well aware of its position in a household.

Preferably, all family members should be dominant over the dog or dogs. This is achieved by behaving in ways that demand deference from the dog. Family members should

TOP: When you play with your dog, it is important that you maintain an upright posture, as in this interaction. If you allow your dog to stand over you, it could interpret this as subordinate behaviour.

Puppies that have not been given clear guidelines about their rank often become aggressive at around 18 months, which is when social maturity is reached (like teenagers testing for feedback on behaviour as they mature).

Scent in your dog's world

The dog has the most sensitive sense of smell of all domestic animals. The nerve cells that detect scent are located in the lining of its nose, which is greatly folded and gives an area of about 150 sq cm (23 sq in), about 30 times that of a human. It also has a far greater concentration of scent-detecting (olfactory) cells – the number varies between breeds, reaching as high as 230 million compared to a human's five million.

As a result, some dogs can detect an odour at up to one millionth of the concentration detectable by a human. When you walk your dog, it is moving through a world of smells, receiving messages via scent at levels as dilute as one in 10,000,000. You cannot even begin to detect them!

Dogs can also detect a wider range of scents than you can. The average human can detect about 1,000 types of scent, and an expert about 4,000, but a dog can detect far more.

Scenting ability varies between breeds, and is best in the hounds that were developed for this purpose. The Bloodhound is one of the best: one animal is known to have

spend time sitting on the dog's bed or in its favourite area. From puppyhood the dog should be fed at least one of its meals after the family has eaten, as this equates to the pack situation where dominant members eat first and subordinates move in later. The dog should be asked to sit and wait while people pass through doorways first. People should maintain an upright posture around the dog. If you lie on the floor and allow the dog to stand over you (as children often do in play), your dog will interpret this as subordinate behaviour – this could lead to aggression from the dog should you later try to dominate it.

ABOVE AND TOP: In a dog's scent-oriented world, urine carries important messages. For this reason, dogs frequently urinate over the spot chosen by predecessors in order to leave behind their own 'signature'.

tracked the scent trail left by a man's feet, through leather-soled boots, four and a half days after it had been laid.

Scent is a very important means of communication for the dog. Glands that secrete odiferous substances are located around the head, neck and groin area, which is why dogs sniff at these areas when they meet.

Two major glands (anal glands) situated on each side of the anus produce a strong-smelling secretion that coats the faeces, leaving a scent message for other dogs (which can persist for quite some time in the environment). These secretions are different in each individual. When your dog sniffs at faeces on the roadside, it is learning about the social status of whoever left the faeces and the time at which they were left.

Urine is also full of information for your dog: who passed by, how long ago, and what is their reproductive status.

The scent organs of the dog

SINUS CAVITIES

BRAIN

OLFACTORY BULB

OLFACTORY EPITHELIUM

HARD PALATE

TONGUE

TOP: Searching for illegal drugs is only one way in which dogs serve humans with their noses. Sniffer dogs also follow scents in search of earthquake, avalanche or mountain accident victims; some even detect mould in timber yards.

Sight in your dog's world

A dog's vision matures at four months. Before this, many objects may appear blurred, which could explain the apparently unprovoked fearful behaviour seen in some puppies.

In most breeds, the eyes are set to the side of the head, so their binocular vision is over a narrower field than ours (about 20° less). The degree of binocular vision varies between breeds because of variations in the positions of the eyes.

Although dogs' binocular vision is not as good as ours, they have much wider peripheral vision (about 70° more), which gives them a greater awareness of movement. They can detect movements so subtle that they would have to be magnified 10 times before a human could see them.

Visual signals are important in canine communication. Posture, ear position, tail position and movement and hair pattern communicate mood and intention.

Your dog will react to subtle changes in body language (in both humans and canines) that you don't even notice. This may explain why your dog suddenly growls at an approaching stranger. Their body language may appear normal to you, but threatening to the dog.

Dogs have rudimentary colour vision that allows them to pick out objects based on colour – shades of colour, however, are not well discriminated.

150°

145°

275°

130°

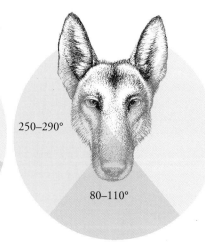

250–290°

80–110°

A HUMAN SEES FROM SIDE-TO-SIDE – A TOTAL OF 150°– OF WHICH 145° IS BINOCULAR OVERLAP.

A CAT SEES FROM SIDE-TO-SIDE – A TOTAL OF 275°– OF WHICH 130° IS BINOCULAR OVERLAP.

A DOG HAS A TOTAL VISION OF 250–290°, WITH 80–110° OF OVERLAP – MUCH LESS THAN THAT OF HUMANS.

TOP: There's no need to pick a particularly bright frisbee for your dog: shades of brightness are not readily discerned, but the movement is easily followed.

Hearing in your dog's world

Communication using sound (vocal communication) is important for dogs, especially in situations where vision is impaired, such as in thick undergrowth. Dogs make a number of different noises, such as whining, barking, growling, howling and grunting, which are used in different contexts.

Compared to humans, dogs have far better hearing. Sound travels in waves, where frequency is measured in units called Hertz (Hz). The higher the frequency, the higher the pitch of the sound.

The average human has a hearing range from 20–20,000Hz. Dogs, on the other hand, have a range of about 20–65,000Hz. They are most sensitive in the range 500–16,000Hz. One reason why some dogs (and cats) dislike the sound of vacuum cleaners or certain two-stroke engines could be that the machines emit disturbing high-pitched sounds that we cannot hear.

'Silent' dog whistles are so called because they emit high-pitched sounds beyond our range of hearing.

The magnitude (loudness) of sounds is measured in decibels (dB) – zero decibels start at the threshold of human hearing. Rustling leaves, for example, measure about 10dB, a whisper 35dB, a motor vehicle 50–60dB, a chain saw 110dB and a jet engine 140dB. Very loud noise can 'hurt' your ears, and the pain threshold for humans is 120dB.

Because their hearing is more acute, dogs can hear much fainter sounds than humans can. For example, a sound just audible to a human standing 6m (20ft) away from its source can be heard by most dogs at a distance of 25m (80ft). Dogs pick up the sound of an approaching thunderstorm 10km (6 miles) away, much sooner than we can.

The dog's acute hearing adds to its value as a guard dog and enables it to obey commands over long distances, for example when working stock on the farm. It may also explain why a dog may appear restless and bark for no apparent reason. We can't hear anything, but the dog can.

Dogs are very sensitive to voice tone, and respond best to a quiet, 'happy' voice. This is why a light, soft voice should be used for praise and a deep, gruff or loud tone for commands or correction. Words used for praise or commands should be short, simple and clear (see pp56–63, Training your dog).

A sound stimulus is reduced in effect if accompanied by touching a dog's body, as the physical stimulus over-rides the auditory command, so don't pat or otherwise touch your dog while you are giving it a command.

With its highly specialised auditory equipment, a dog is able to hear even faint, distant sounds and determine their exact location

THE LARGE OUTER EAR FLAP HAS PRECISE MUSCULAR DIRECTION TO LOCATE SOUND-SOURCES

SEMI-CIRCULAR CANALS

INNER EAR

OSSICLES (HAMMER, ANVIL AND STIRRUP)

COCHLEA

EXTERNAL EAR CANAL

A LARGE TYMPANIC CAVITY ACTS AS A RESONATING CHAMBER AND FURTHER AMPLIFIES SOUND

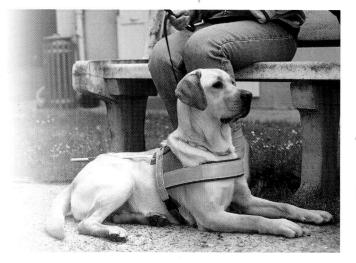

TRAINING YOUR DOG
and your household

Most aspiring dog owners dream of the perfect canine companion: obedient, quiet and well behaved in public. Unfortunately for some, the dream is soon shattered. Their beloved pet takes them for a walk, covers their good clothes with muddy paw prints, chases cats, bowls over elderly pedestrians and cannot be left alone in the car in case it demolishes the upholstery.

How can you avoid finding yourself in this situation? Start training your puppy as soon as you get it.

Remember, though, that dog training must be a partnership. It is not just the dog that needs training, but you and your family as well. It is no good if one member of your family is able to handle a dog properly while none of the others can. All members of your family must be dominant over the dog, although it may single out one individual as its pack leader.

Puppy kindergarten

These kindergartens are usually held in selected areas of veterinary clinics that are free from any possible contamination. They are designed to allow young puppies to socialise in a safe, disease-free environment and to help owners begin training as soon as they bring the puppy home, usually at the age of seven or eight weeks. There is strong evidence to show that puppies that have attended kindergarten are far more obedient and easier to handle than those that have not.

If possible, join a puppy kindergarten as soon as you get the puppy and spend at least 10 minutes twice a day reinforcing and practising what you learn each week.

Once you have completed puppy kindergarten, keep at your daily practice sessions. By this time your puppy will have had all its vaccinations and you will be taking it out and about. Practise all your training at regular intervals during walks, too.

If you want to complete further training, locate a reputable dog training centre (see p63, Advanced training).

Basic training at home

Puppy kindergarten will offer basic training, but you may wish to start training your dog at home while you are waiting for the kindergarten classes to begin. Puppies learn very quickly from eight weeks of age. Most can master the four easiest commands – 'sit', 'stay', 'come', 'down' and 'heel' – by the time they are three months.

Most puppies will work for food treats. Dried liver is popular. Puppies that don't like liver may work for cheese or biscuits.

It is best to use treats all the time in the early stages of training. Gradually, you can use them intermittently and eventually phase them out, rewarding with praise only.

TOP: The first guide dogs were trained by the German government after the First World War to help blinded soldiers. Labrador Retrievers are the most popular assistance dogs today.
TOP RIGHT: A soft harness and leash for puppies and small dogs.

The basic commands

Teach the commands in the order in which they are listed here, as 'sit' is usually the most easily learned command, and 'come' is the most difficult. It is best to train a puppy on a leash.

Sit: Stand in front of the puppy, hold a treat above its head, just about at ear level. Ask it to sit. To get the treat the puppy needs to put its head up and back, and in doing this it will naturally place its bottom on the ground. As soon as this happens, give it the treat and praise it.

Some puppies will walk backwards instead of sitting. If you have this problem, stand the puppy in a corner before asking it to sit. Most learn very quickly and can sit well after only one week of training.

Down: Ask the puppy to sit and reward it when it does so. Hold another reward in your hand and move it between the puppy's front legs and under its chest, giving the command 'down'. In following the treat with its nose the puppy will move into a lying position. When it has done this, release the treat and praise the puppy.

Some puppies only get half way to the ground at first. If this happens, use your free hand to gently push the puppy on the shoulder until it lies down.

Stay: Ask the puppy to sit or lie down. Then stand beside it and place one hand flat in front of its face. Give the command 'stay', take one step forward, stop, then step back again and praise the puppy.

Very gradually increase the number of steps you take away from the puppy. If the puppy moves, say 'no', place it straight back in position and ask it to stay again. In two to three weeks, practicing daily, the puppy should stay happily while you walk to the opposite end of the room and return to it.

Heel: From its sitting position, encourage the puppy to look up at you by holding a treat in your clenched hand and talking in an 'interesting' voice. This means varying the tone and pitch and saying things that will make you feel very silly!

Walk forward, give the command 'heel', and encourage the puppy to follow while still looking up at you. Always

Teach your puppy to 'sit' and 'down', using a treat and praise

SIT: TELL YOUR PUPPY TO 'SIT', MOTIONING IT DOWNWARDS WITH A TREAT JUST ABOVE EAR LEVEL. THEN REWARD IT WITH THE TREAT AND PRAISE.

DOWN: TELL YOUR PUPPY TO 'SIT', THEN REWARD IT. NEXT, MOVE ANOTHER TREAT BETWEEN THE PUPPY'S FRONT LEGS AND UNDER ITS CHEST, GIVING THE COMMAND 'DOWN'. GIVE THE PUPPY THE TREAT AND PRAISE IT.

TOP: The 'sit' command is easiest to learn and, therefore, usually the first one taught. A puppy will respond enthusiastically to positive learning experiences and, by the age of three months, should obey 'stay' as well.

keep the lead loose. Never resort to pulling the puppy along after you. Keep repeating 'heel, good dog, look'. When the puppy is walking freely looking up, give it a reward but keep walking while you do so. This reinforces that the reward is for walking well. If you stop to give the reward, the puppy will associate stopping with a treat and will soon refuse to move!

Come: Practise this frequently throughout the day in various situations. Always carry treats. Call the puppy by name, followed by the command 'come', and reward it with a treat when it comes to you. When you call, you need to sound interesting enough to override the rest of the environment.

When the puppy comes to you, treat it as the most wonderful event of the day. You have to make it worth the puppy's while to return to you when there are so many other interesting things to investigate.

Always take young puppies and dogs out on an extending leash and do not let them run totally free in public areas until you know they will return. This can take up to a year of training. It is one of the most difficult lessons for the puppy.

It is essential that you never, ever punish the puppy for not returning. If it ignores you, quietly go and get it (if you are working free at home in an enclosed space) or reel in the extending lead. Ask the puppy to sit, then reward

and praise it for that. Have a game, and make following you fun.

Keep trying and eventually your perseverance will be rewarded.

Quiet: Some dogs have a tendency to bark at the slightest provocation. It is useful to teach these dogs a 'quiet' command.

Start this training when the dog is sitting or lying quietly. Praise it and say 'quiet'. Do this frequently through the day. When the dog barks at something, call it to you, ask it to sit, then tell it to be quiet. Praise and reward it for being quiet.

As it is natural for a dog to bark at unfamiliar sounds or intruders, this command will control barking, but not extinguish in the dog the desire to bark.

Fetch: Some dog breeds are natural retrievers, while others just do not see the point. It should be evident from about 12 weeks old if your puppy is going to enjoy retrieving – it will naturally pick up objects and invite you to chase it while holding something in its mouth. If you throw something such as a ball, your puppy will chase it and try to pick it up.

The modern method of enticing a puppy to obey 'stay' and 'heel'

STAY: TELL YOUR PUPPY TO 'SIT' AND THEN 'STAY', USING A TREAT AND PRAISE. REPEAT THE 'STAY' COMMAND AND STEP AWAY. REPEAT THE PROCESS ONCE MORE.

HEEL: ENCOURAGE THE SITTING PUPPY TO LOOK AT YOU BY HOLDING A TREAT. THEN WALK AND ENCOURAGE YOUR PUPPY TO FOLLOW, REPEATING THE COMMAND 'HEEL'. GIVE IT A TREAT WHILE IT IS WALKING FREELY, LOOKING UP.

TOP: A soft muzzle can be used on walks and during training to prevent a dog from biting others.

You need to work with this natural retrieve drive to teach the dog to fetch an object on command and to relinquish it to you. Begin by encouraging the puppy to chase a toy that is hand held, then thrown a short distance. Go with the puppy, pick up the toy, give it to the puppy and take the puppy back to the starting point. Give the command 'fetch'.

Work with the puppy on an extending leash at first so that you have control over its movements.

Some puppies retrieve the object but then refuse to give it up afterwards. You can overcome this by swapping the retrieved object for a treat or a brief play with a favourite toy. Eventually, the fun of having an object thrown for chasing is enough reward to encourage the puppy to give up the object.

Breeds that are natural retrievers include all the 'bird' dogs such as Labradors, Pointers, Setters and Poodles. Other breeds that like to retrieve include German Shepherd Dogs, Dalmatians, most Terriers and many cross-breeds.

Control of mouthing and play-biting

Puppies often bite in play with people, just as they do with other puppies. This play-biting can become difficult to cope with, especially in puppies that do not attend a puppy kindergarten.

During puppy play, if one puppy bites another too hard, the bitten puppy will cry out sharply and will immediately turn its back on the biter and refuse to interact further. If pushed, it may growl or snap at the biter, but this is not usually necessary. Usually the biter will appear shocked by the other puppy's reaction and will back off. Further approaches will be gentler. If your

puppy bites you, say 'ouch!' loudly and walk away. Ignore the biting puppy or, if possible, leave the room for five minutes. Return, call the puppy, and ask it to sit and then pat it. If it bites again, repeat the process. From this treatment your puppy will soon discover that biting causes it to be left alone and ignored.

Some puppies will continue to bite despite this treatment. These puppies may need to be physically placed in a subordinate position to make a point. This is done by gently rolling the puppy onto one side, holding it down with one hand and holding its mouth closed with the other, while looking directly into its eyes. When the puppy stops struggling, release it and stroke it gently. Repeat this procedure whenever the puppy bites hard and refuses to stop.

It is probably a good idea to ask your vet or behaviourist to demonstrate this before you attempt it yourself.

Avoid 'roughing up the puppy' as an attempt to play. This will only encourage the puppy to bite and play roughly. If you must indulge in tugging and growling games, use a tug toy and do not allow the puppy to latch onto sleeves or trousers.

ABOVE: A soft clip-on collar and leash for a small to medium-sized dog.
TOP: Although Rottweilers are not natural retrievers, they can still be trained to fetch on command, an important obedience exercise for such a powerful animal.

Jumping up

Some dogs become very excited when visitors arrive or when owners return home, and express this by jumping up at the person or people present. This can be irritating and may result in clothing being torn or damaged – and, of course, it may result in young children or frail older people being knocked over.

If your dog jumps up, turn right away and walk in the opposite direction. Do not speak to the dog and, if possible, leave the room and shut in the dog. Return to the dog and immediately ask it to sit. Reward the sit with a treat. If it jumps up again, say 'no'. Ask it to sit and again reward the sit. If the dog jumps and manages to get its paws onto you, turn away again without touching the dog, so that it falls to the ground. Request it to sit again and reward the dog.

If the dog insists on jumping despite this protocol, enlist help. Arrange for someone to visit at a pre-arranged time. Have the dog on a head halter and lead, and prevent the dog from jumping at the visitor. Command the dog to sit calmly while the visitor enters the house and greets you.

The visitor should ignore the dog at first. Reward the dog for quiet behaviour, then allow the visitor to greet the dog while it is sitting calmly. If it makes any attempt to jump, the visitor should stop petting it and walk away. Once the dog is sitting quietly, the visitor may return and pet the dog.

Family members can help each other in a similar way if the dog is a problem every time someone returns home. Dogs soon learn that they will be ignored or shut away if they jump, and will usually change their behaviour to running up and sitting in front of a visitor or their returning owner.

Preventing jumping up:
○ Do not encourage puppies to stand up on you or jump up at you for attention.
○ Don't be over exuberant in greeting your dog or puppy.
○ Command the dog to sit or lie down before you give it attention.

Reprimand and correction

Modern training techniques rarely involve physical correction: their emphasis is on redirecting unacceptable behaviour and rewarding correct behaviour. This is known as positive reinforcement.

'Traditional' methods of hitting dogs with rolled up newspapers or slapping them may result in dogs that are hand shy and confused. Remember that in most cases the dog is not deliberately behaving badly. Your dog cannot easily tell the difference between the old sneaker that it is allowed to play with and your expensive shoes. Patient redirection to its own toys will be more successful than shouting and hitting the dog.

If you really feel physical correction is indicated and redirection has not worked – for example, if the dog insists on cornering the cat or tearing up the cushions – then the following 'correction procedure' is far better than striking the animal:
○ Take hold of it firmly by the collar.
○ Look directly into its eyes.

TOP: Jumping up is unacceptable behaviour and can be dangerous – prevent this by never being too enthusiastic when greeting your dog or puppy on your return home.

- Say 'no' firmly.
- Banish it to another room.
- Return to the dog in two minutes, request a 'sit' or 'down', and reward it.

A water pistol may also be used to correct this sort of behaviour. Squirt the dog full in the face while it is performing the behaviour. When it jumps back in surprise, call it to you, request a sit and reward it.

In most cases, if the dog has been properly trained as a puppy using redirection and reward, physical correction should not be required.

Remember that there are veterinarians and behaviourists that specialise in behaviour problems. If at any stage you are having difficulty with training your dog, or if it is aggressive, pushy, noisy, excessively fearful or anxious, help is readily available.

Training aids

Your puppy should be fitted with a soft puppy collar as soon as it has settled into your home. Start by putting the collar on for short periods at a time when your puppy is playing or eating, then gradually extend its use until it is being worn all the time.

Once the puppy is used to the collar, clip on a lightweight, 120cm (47in) leash. Practice walking the puppy around for a short period, when necessary using a gentle pull to steer it in the right direction. Try to keep your puppy on your left side, holding the handle of the leash in your right hand. Be patient while the puppy gets used to this, and use lots of praise and rewards when it does things right.

If the puppy resents the leash, try leaving it clipped to its collar and trailing behind the puppy for short periods – just remember to follow the puppy to make sure the leash doesn't catch on anything or end up being chewed.

Once your puppy is used to walking with you around the garden on a collar and lead, try a trip around the neighbourhood. Forget about making the puppy walk on your left side all the time, as it is now being exposed to new experiences and should be allowed some freedom to investigate.

A long leash is important, because it allows your puppy freedom to investigate the environment while safely under your control. Keeping it on a tight leash may cause it to back away rather than follow you willingly.

Standard leashes and collars

From six months onwards, adolescent and adult dogs may wear broad nylon or leather collars. It is wise to attach an identity disc to these.

Choose a leash that is suitable for the size and strength of your dog. For a large breed it is better to have a fairly short, strong leash, with the handle made of a leather and a chain attachment to the collar, or a short rolled-leather leash. For a small breed you can use a thinner, longer lead made of leather or nylon.

Expanding leashes

These come in a range of sizes correlated to the weight of the dog. They provide a leash length of 3–5m (10–15ft) and are ideal for training young dogs to return when called, as they allow controlled freedom.

Important: It is best not to use any of the following aids, such as head halters, harnesses and chokers, without expert

ABOVE: A light-weight expanding or retractable leash.
TOP: A soft nylon, quick-release collar and leash for a medium-sized dog.

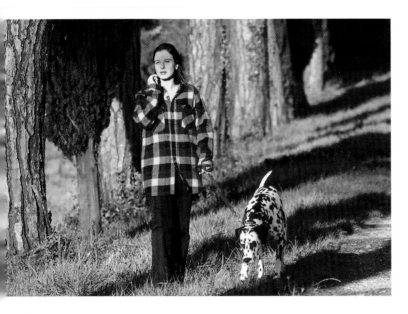

immediately release it. The dog learns to associate the noise of the chain with discomfort if it pulls, so it walks without pulling. Chains with large links are preferable to those with small links.

The trouble is that many people link the choker incorrectly. Have your veterinarian show you the right way. Another problem is that dogs ignore the sound and pull hard on the chain. When they do this, the chain tightens and they literally choke themselves. Double-action slip-chains are also available, which tighten only a little and do not choke the dog. Or you can use a slip-collar made of leather, cord or a broad strip of nylon.

Warning: Improperly used, these chains can seriously damage the throat or neck vertebrae.

advice. Check with your veterinarian as to which, if any, is appropriate for your dog. Make sure that you take the dog in for a proper fitting and instructions on use.

Head halters

Some dogs insist on pulling when on a leash, which makes walking them unpleasant. Head halters are designed to allow you to control the dog's head, and therefore its speed and direction.

Head halters are also useful in helping you to avoid aggressive encounters between dogs. With a halter you can turn your dog's head away from an approaching dog. This should stop any aggression because you are placing your dog into a submissive posture.

Warning: If you wish to control your dog with a head halter you must learn to use it properly. Tugging too hard could cause damage to your dog's neck.

Check, choker or slip-chains

These are chains that are looped to form a slip-noose effect. The idea is to tighten the chain with a short, sharp jerk and

Harnesses

These are designed to fit around the dog's chest and behind its front legs. They can be very useful for small dogs, especially those with short faces, or for dogs that have had neck injuries.

A standard harness is useless on a large dog with a tendency to pull; rather choose a 'no-pull' harness, designed to put pressure on the dog's chest and to pull its front leg back when it pulls. It is usually quite effective, although it can cause chafing.

Citronella collars

These collars are fitted with a device that sprays citronella into the dog's face each time it barks, and can be useful in some cases of nuisance barking. It is important that the dog be assessed by a behaviourist before one is used, and then the collar should at first be used only under supervision. If the barking is anxiety-related, using a citronella collar will make the dog much worse.

ABOVE LEFT: A choker, also known as a check or slip-chain, for a medium-sized dog.
ABOVE RIGHT: A harness for a medium-sized dog.
TOP: Once your dog can walk sensibly alongside you, you may wish to consider more advanced training.

Advanced training

Once it has mastered the basic commands, you will have a dog that is manageable and fun to be with. You can then build on these and teach distance commands, such as asking the dog to obey 'down' from a distance. Dog training schools and clubs can help you with advanced training, and your veterinarian should be able to provide recommendations.

Some breeds ideal for working, obedience or agility trials

Bearded Collie

Belgian Shepherd

Border Collie

Boxer

Dalmatian

Doberman

German Shepherd Dog (Alsatian)

Golden Retriever

Great Dane

Irish Setter

Labrador Retriever

Old English Sheepdog

Pointer

Poodle

Rottweiler

Schnauzer

Weimaraner

Welsh Corgi

Training the adult dog

If you adopt a dog from an animal shelter, you will be faced with training an adult animal. It may have bad habits that have been established over months or years. Time, effort and patience will be required to retrain it to behave in a way that is acceptable to you, but it can be done. For example, police dogs often do not begin training until they are 20 months of age.

ABOVE: Very large dogs are suitable only for people who are able to provide the space, time and patience needed to train and exercise them every day. In many countries it is now law that large dogs be muzzled when walking in public places.

In general, the training will be little different from that used with puppies, although you should follow the same protocols for the various commands as described for puppy training. Be aware, though, that the dog may have had some prior training and may respond to different commands, so play with words for a while and evaluate the response. For example, some dogs lie down to a 'drop' command, while others respond to 'down' or 'lie down'.

Difficulties may arise if a command has become obsolete. This happens where people use a command but do not ensure that a suitable response occurs. The dog then learns to ignore the command. This commonly occurs with 'no' and 'come'. In such cases it is often better to use alternative words to train the dog to respond; you might choose 'stop' and 'here' instead.

Once you have decided on a particular command, ensure that a response always occurs. Keep your new dog on a retractable leash until you know that it responds well to your chosen commands.

House training can be a major problem with some adult dogs. Those that have been rescued from inferior breeding kennels may have become used to defecating on concrete (they have developed a 'substrate preference') and as a result will soil footpaths, driveways and doorsteps, to your and the neighbours' annoyance. If there is a solid surface indoors they may be stimulated to defecate on it, too.

You need to change their substrate preference. The only way to do this is to keep a strict eye on such a dog, take it outside on a leash whenever it is likely to need to relieve itself, stay with it, and praise it when it has obliged in a suitable area.

Do not expect your dog to know what is expected of it automatically. Just because it is an adult doesn't mean it comes ready-programmed to suit your requirements! Don't demand too much too soon and be understanding if it makes mistakes.

Guarding

Most dogs of either sex have some tendency to guard their home territory. Motivation to guard varies between breeds. Rottweilers, German Shepherd Dogs, Dobermans and Rhodesian Ridgebacks are among those most likely to guard. Males tend to guard at a higher intensity than females.

Most people feel secure with a dog that will warn them of the presence of an intruder by barking. A dog may be encouraged to do this by the owner reacting to noises outside the house. If the owner jumps up, goes to the door and says to the dog 'What's that, what's that?' or makes a hissing noise, the dog will be encouraged to bark. Dogs that have been trained to obey voice commands should

ABOVE: Police dogs receive highly specialised training and need to be courageous as well as intelligent. Formal training usually only begins when the dog is emotionally mature.
TOP: A leather collar, a strong, yet soft, cloth leash and choker chain for a large dog.

area. They are potentially dangerous and owners risk legal action if a person is injured. These dogs cannot tell the difference between someone calling at the property for legitimate reasons and someone with evil intent. All intruders will be bitten.

The arrival of a new baby

About two months prior to the baby's arrival, or as soon as you have set up the nursery, introduce your dog to the equipment and toys that will be part of the nursery scene. Allow it to become familiar with the scent of the talcs and lotions you will be using on your newborn, and to the sounds of squeaky toys and musical night-lights.

While you are in hospital after the birth, send used baby clothes home with your partner and let the dog sniff them to become familiar with their scent. When you bring the infant home, have a relative hold it in the hall while you greet your dog alone. Leash the dog, ask your partner to hold the leash and bring in the infant. Allow the dog to sniff the infant and accompany you to the nursery while you settle the infant into its crib.

In the days that follow, allow the dog to be involved with all the baby care. It is best to have it tied up close by in the room while you are busy changing or feeding. Never leave the dog and infant together unsupervised. Infants move and sound like prey and can evoke predatory aggression in some dogs (see p69, Predatory aggression).

stop reacting to an intruder when reassured or given the commands 'sit' or 'quiet' by their owner.

Dogs may be trained to attack on command, but this is not something the general public should need or wish to do. Training dogs in this area is a specialised, professional job.

Some people want to have dogs that attack intruders on sight. In most cases these dogs are kept in outdoor compounds and are encouraged to react without any control at the first sign of intrusion. These dogs are allowed to bite anyone entering the

ABOVE: While toddlers and dogs can become the best of friends, it is essential that you never leave an infant and dog alone together.
TOP: If your dog is consistently vicious towards people, it may be seized and taken away by the local animal control department.

BEHAVIOUR PROBLEMS
and how to deal with them

Aggression

In the canine world, aggression is part of normal behaviour. Dogs display aggression when threatened by another animal, during hunting, when protecting their young and when establishing a social order, and show it by adopting various postures accompanied by vocalisations such as growling, snarling and barking. Aggression between dogs may be counteracted by submissive behaviour by the weaker or lower-ranking animal. This helps to avoid serious fights.

Aggression can become a problem when it is excessive, or directed towards people. In fact, it is one of the most common behaviour problems seen in dogs.

Dominance aggression

This is the most common type of aggression problem and occurs when a dog tries to enforce its will on its owners, challenging them for control. The dog may already feel that it is in control, or it may be testing its owner to get some feedback on its standing in the household.

Dominantly aggressive dogs commonly growl or snap at their owners if they are disturbed while sleeping, or asked to move from a specific spot or to obey a command that does not appeal to them. This form of aggression is usually first seen when the dog reaches social maturity, at the age of 18 months to two years. At this age the animal needs to know where it stands in the hierarchy of the household and will attempt to establish a 'rank'. As a result, it may growl at some members of a family but not others. Children are usually the first to be challenged, probably because they are small and less assertive in manner than adults.

Dogs with dominance aggression may also show possessive aggression and/or food aggression (see p68).

If your dog is behaving in an aggressive manner towards you or members of your family, you should seek the help of your veterinarian. He or she may then refer you to an animal behaviour specialist.

The dog must have a preliminary health check to make sure that there is no underlying health problem causing the change in behaviour. If the dog is diagnosed with dominance aggression, there are special behaviour modification programmes that need to be followed. These are usually highly successful, but require time, effort and motivation on the owner's part.

Preventing dominance aggression: You can reduce the risk of your dog developing dominance aggression by providing it with clear guidelines for acceptable behaviour from early in puppyhood. Overleaf are some helpful guidelines:

TOP: If you want to be the least favourite member of your neighbourhood, allow your dog to bark uncontrollably! Barking is the behaviour least tolerated by non-dog owners and owners alike.

- Feed your puppy its evening meal after the family has eaten. This reinforces the family's dominance over the puppy. In a pack situation, dominant animals eat first.
- Make sure that you sit on the puppy's bed for a short while every day, to assert your dominance.
- Begin training as soon as you get the puppy, by attending puppy kindergarten.
- If the puppy shows signs of aggression, give it time out for five or 10 minutes in a separate room. Play with it only when it is behaving non-aggressively.
- Require that the puppy allow family members to walk through doorways ahead of it.
- Spend five or 10 minutes daily on training.
- Insist on 'sit' and 'down' at least twice daily once the puppy has mastered these commands.
- Do not give in to pawing for attention. Ignore it and provide attention only when the puppy is quiet or has earned attention by sitting when asked.

Fear aggression

This is the second-most common type of aggression, and in some cases it is inherited. Fear aggression is most common in dogs adopted from animal shelters and often stems from past abuses. These animals require rehabilitation.

Dogs with fear aggression may start to show typical behaviour patterns from three months. They appear scared even when there is nothing to trigger the fear. When out walking they may appear terrified of an approaching pedestrian, or of an object on the roadside. They respond by growling, shaking, tucking their tails between their legs, backing away from the object or person, and possibly urinating or defecating. The hair on their neck and rump will usually be erect.

With these animals it is important to seek help from an animal behaviour specialist. They often require medication and a programme of desensitisation, which may involve gradual exposure to the triggering stimuli, in conjunction with relaxation therapy. In the meantime, try these temporary measures:

- Avoid contact with stimuli that trigger a fear response until help can be found.
- Don't reward the fearful behaviour by patting and reassuring the dog. If it starts to behave fearfully, ignore it.
- When it starts to relax, reward the relaxed behaviour

Preventing fear aggression: It is probably impossible to prevent fear aggression completely in genetically predisposed animals. Early exposure to different environments and people and positive experiences associated with these may help.

ABOVE: Play fights are a method of establishing which dog is dominant, without causing serious injury.

Possessive aggression

A typical example is a dog that refuses to relinquish toys or objects stolen from its owners. When pressed to return these items, it may growl, snarl and even bite. Dogs showing possessive aggression often also show dominance aggression. The possessive aggression is considered to be part of a 'control complex' in these animals.

Possessive aggression is potentially dangerous, especially where young children associate with the animal. Your behaviourist can recommend a programme for treatment, and until you have completed that programme it is safer not to meet the dog's challenge.

Preventing possessive aggression: These tactics are sure to help:

○ Ensure that puppies are given a clear understanding of their subordinate position in the household (see p66, Dominance aggression).
○ Avoid playing fighting games over toys with young puppies or older dogs.
○ Teach puppies to relinquish balls or toys in exchange for rewards.

Food aggression

Dogs showing food aggression may be very dangerous, especially for young children. These dogs savagely defend their food and growl constantly while eating. If they have a bone or a biscuit, they will sometimes even lunge at and bite anyone who passes close to them.

Food aggression may occur in conjunction with dominance aggression.

It is probably easiest and safest to feed these dogs in a separate and enclosed room. Avoid giving them bones as these are usually very actively defended. It is possible, but often difficult, to train them out of this behaviour, so seek expert help.

Start by asking the dog to sit at a distance from its empty food bowl. Pick up the empty bowl, place a little food in it, place it on the ground and allow the dog to eat. When the dog has finished, repeat the process. Eventually you should be able to hold the bowl while the dog eats from it.

If the dog growls during any part of the procedure, stop the feeding.

States of aggression response

NORMAL DOCILE STATE

BEGINNINGS OF AGGRESSION

INCREASED AGGRESSION

FIERCE AGGRESSION

States of aggression and fear response

BEGINNINGS OF FEAR

INCREASED FEARFUL RESPONSE

AGGRESSION AND FEAR

FEAR AND EXTREME AGGRESSION

ABOVE: Fear can produce an aggressive response in dogs. The above sequences show the progressive stages, from an initially docile or slightly fearful state to fierce aggression or fear and extreme aggression.

Preventing food aggression: Food aggression is normal behaviour because it is natural for dogs to protect their food. Puppies in large litters may rapidly learn to fight for a larger portion, and to guard whatever they have.

It may be helpful to hand feed your new puppy frequently from its own bowl and to sit nearby while it eats. Make sure that your dog is in no doubt that you are dominant.

Maternal aggression

This occurs close to, or immediately after whelping. Bitches will savagely defend their puppies in response to any intrusion, and on occasion have even killed their puppies.

Maternal aggression may also occur during false pregnancy when there is no prospect of puppies and toys are protected instead. Try these tactics to deal with maternal aggression:

○ Try to avoid disturbing the bitch during the first week of motherhood.

○ From then on, call her out of the room, attach a lead and walk her while someone else changes the bedding.

○ Feed her on return and leave her alone.

○ In cases of false pregnancy, remove the nest and toys while the bitch is out walking. Alter her daily routine and provide new interests. Some bitches may need hormone treatment.

Preventing maternal aggression: Bitches showing this behaviour should be spayed as they are likely to behave this way with future litters and there appears to be an inherited tendency for this behaviour.

Predatory aggression

Dogs prone to predatory aggression will develop a habit of stalking and killing other animals, such as cats, squirrels and even chickens, sheep and goats. In most cases this is done silently and swiftly. Not only is this highly undesirable behaviour, as these dogs will kill neighbours' pets as well as wildlife, it is a potential threat for humans.

The worst possible situation is when such a dog begins to focus its attention on children and babies.

To the dog, newborn and young babies appear to be behaving like wounded prey: they are uncoordinated and

prone to sudden high-pitched screaming. Such actions may trigger a dog's predatory behaviour.

A dog showing this behaviour cannot be trained out of it, and must be under control at all times. It should never be left unsupervised around children.

Preventing predatory aggression: Good obedience training will help to control these animals, but they can't be trusted to be alone with possible victims.

ABOVE: Maternal aggression decreases in intensity as the puppies get older.
TOP CENTRE: It is natural for dogs to jealously guard their food or bones and fight for larger portions.

Redirected aggression

This behaviour is seen when a dog is prevented from doing something aggressive that its owners consider inappropriate: for example, growling at a visitor or terrorising the mailman. Immediately after it has been reprimanded the dog chases the cat or threatens a family member.

The most important thing with this type of aggression is to identify what triggers the behaviour and deal with that. If the dog bites the cat every time it is told off for chasing the mailman, then it is best for everyone if the dog learns not to chase the person who delivers the mail. This involves a process of desensitisation to his or her arrival.

In order to achieve this, the dog is taught to associate the mail deliverer with another behaviour, such as 'sit and concentrate on the owner', in return for a food reward. A behaviourist will help you with a protocol designed for your dog.

Preventing redirected aggression: It is probably impossible to predict if an animal will show redirected aggression. Thorough obedience training should help to decrease the likelihood of this behaviour occurring.

If a dog shows signs of inappropriate aggression towards any other animal or person, squirting it with a water pistol may help diffuse the situation until a behaviour modification programme can be started.

Idiopathic aggression

'Idiopathic' means of unknown cause. Some dogs may suddenly, and for no obvious reason, have violent aggressive outbursts. Such dogs may foam at the mouth during these outbursts and cannot be distracted or safely approached. In these animals it is likely that there is some underlying mental defect. This is a difficult condition to deal with. These dogs are best shut away during such outbursts, if possible, and may require sedation. In some instances, your vet may suggest euthanasia.

ABOVE: Highly dangerous predatory aggression can be controlled with obedience training.
TOP: Inter-dog aggression is a common problem on walks – it may be due to underlying anxiety in the dog.

Preventing idiopathic aggression: The behaviour cannot be predicted, as there are usually no obvious triggers, so it is impossible to prevent. Fortunately, the condition is relatively rare.

Aggression towards strange dogs

This commonly causes problems on walks. Two dogs, on or off leashes, meet and begin to fight. An aggressive dog will challenge any dog that crosses its path, making this challenge regardless of the age, sex or size of the perceived opponent.

If the other dog is extremely submissive, the situation may be diffused. If not, or in some cases despite a submissive display by the other dog, there may be a seriously aggressive encounter.

This is frightening for the owners of both dogs, and often physically damaging to the dogs involved. It is no fun to walk a dog that is constantly and overtly aggressive to every other dog it encounters. These dogs are behaving abnormally. The behaviour may be due to an underlying anxiety, and a lack of certain chemicals in the brain.

Where this behaviour occurs in male dogs, castration may be helpful. It will not, on its own, solve the problem, but will help by decreasing the dog's reactivity.

It is helpful to walk an aggressive dog in a head halter (see p62, Training your dog). This ensures that you have all-important control of the dog's head. When another dog approaches, turn your dog's head to the side. This puts it in a submissive posture with the neck exposed and prevents aggressive signalling.

There are desensitisation programmes which may be used to modify this behaviour. These involve working in groups of dogs. Aggressive dogs are taught to relax and concentrate on their owners in the presence of other dogs. Ask your veterinarian to recommend an animal behaviourist, who will be able to help you with this. Your dog may require medication.

Preventing aggression towards strange dogs:

- Castration decreases the level of aggression in males.
- Adequate socialisation of dogs from puppyhood may be helpful. Personal experience suggests that dogs that have socialised regularly and positively with other dogs from puppyhood, and continue to do so through adulthood, are less likely to show inappropriate aggression towards strange dogs.

Aggression between dogs in the same household

Dogs living in the same household need to have a hierarchy – in other words, they need to establish an order of dominance. Problems often arise when a new puppy, introduced to a household with an older resident dog, reaches social maturity: any time from 18 months to two years of age (the teenage years!). At this age, it will begin to challenge the older dog. It may try to take over a preferred sleeping place or a favourite toy, for example. Fights will start if the older dog does not wish to give way.

It is important to decide which dog is likely to win in an aggressive encounter. If the older dog has become feeble and is unlikely to win the next few battles, you need to reinforce the younger dog's bid for dominance, even

TOP: This type of behaviour is a sign that all is well – there is no inter-dog aggression on the horizon. The anal glands give important information about the dog and its sexual and social status.

though you might feel that you are betraying an old friend in some way. You can do this by feeding it first, allowing it access to preferred areas, and giving it attention before the other dog.

If the older dog is still strong, is of a larger breed and is most likely to win any battles, reinforce the older dog's status as just described.

There will be no peace in the household until this problem is sorted out. In situations where both dogs are reasonably equal, you may need to find another home for one of them or they will be constantly fighting. Speak to your behaviourist.

It is important not to leave the two dogs alone together until the hierarchy has been established. Fights in this situation can be quite savage.

Preventing aggression between dogs in the same household: If you decide to have a second dog:

○ Get one of the opposite sex to the resident dog.
○ Do not leave dogs alone together in confined spaces.
○ Do not give bones or biscuits to groups of dogs.

Barking

Barking is probably the dog behaviour least well tolerated by people, especially in suburban areas. Some breeds bark more readily than others. Terriers, for example, bark at the slightest provocation, while Siberian Huskies rarely bark and Basenjis only yodel. It is a natural means of canine communication. In some instances, however, dogs begin to bark excessively and this becomes a serious problem.

There are many potential causes of frequent barking and it is important to establish the cause in each case. The tone and pattern of the barking may provide some clues as to the reason for it. The dog that begins barking as soon as its owner leaves the house, and continues to do so, usually in a monotone, throughout the owner's absence may be suffering from separation anxiety (see p76).

Some dogs bark sporadically throughout the day. This is usually in response to some trigger stimulus such as the movements of neighbours, arrival of the mailman, birds perching on a perimeter fence, or presence of a neighbouring dog.

Some dogs bark and yap excitedly for quite some time when their owners arrive home. This barking is really only a problem if the neighbours are complaining; these dogs are not usually distressed.

ABOVE: Challenges may occur between dogs in the same household, usually in the form of body posture. It is important that you back the dog most likely to win, or there will never be peace in the house.

If your dog is barking during your absence and the neighbours are complaining about the disturbance, try to enlist their help in correcting the problem. Ask them to note down the times at which the dog barks and also how long it barks. If the dog is barking continuously until you return, it may be suffering from separation anxiety. This is a serious behaviour problem and you will need the help of an animal behaviourist.

If the dog barks at the person who delivers the mail, at passers-by in general, or when neighbours come and go, try leaving the dog inside with toys and a comfortable bed so that it is not so easily stimulated by these events. If you know that you will have to leave the dog for a while, make sure it has had a long run or a vigorous play session before you leave. It is much more likely to relax and sleep while you are out if it is tired.

Dogs that bark while their owners are at home can be trained to be quiet on command. Such dogs can also be 'desensitised' to triggers such as doorbells and mailmen.

There are training aids such as collars that are triggered to release citronella spray when the dog barks. These may be useful for some animals (see p62, Training your dog).

Preventing problem barking:

○ Train your puppy to respond to a 'Quiet!' command (see p58, Training).

○ Expose your puppy or new dog to as many unusual sights and sounds as possible, as frequently as possible and reward it for calm behaviour at this time.

○ When your dog or puppy becomes over excited and excessively vocal, redirect its behaviour by asking it to sit or lie down for a reward. Try to get it to concentrate on you and a food treat and ignore the stimulus that caused the barking.

Destructive behaviour

Destructive behaviour is very much more common in young dogs. Puppies need to chew, especially during teething, as this soothes their aching or itching gums – it is also a way of exploring and investigating their worlds. Older dogs may also be destructive. This may be play related or, if it happens while the dog is left alone, may be due to separation anxiety (see p76).

Puppies can be very destructive if not managed properly. If your puppy starts to chew furniture or doors, tell it 'no'

ABOVE: Puppies are capable of displaying inter-dog aggression, just like adult dogs.

Digging

Dogs dig to bury a toy or a bone, to uncover something they can smell or that they know to have been buried, to make a hole in which they can keep warm or cool off, or simply to play. Soil is fun because it moves and changes. They may also dig to escape under a fence.

Digging can cause problems where the dog is forever digging up recently planted or carefully nurtured gardens, or managing to escape by tunnelling under fences.

If a dog digs obsessively and cannot be distracted from the behaviour it may be suffering from an obsessive-compulsive disorder (see p77). This needs to be dealt with by an animal behaviourist.

If your dog is digging in unacceptable areas, redirect it to an area that is its own. This might be a sandpit or a waste area of the garden.

If the dog persists in digging in the unacceptable area, you could try burying inflated balloons in the region, or investing in snappy trainers, which are a little like plastic mousetraps. These snappy trainers are triggered by the digging and fly up with a snapping noise, which startles the dog.

Digging beneath fences can be successfully prevented by electrifying the fence with a suitable voltage. (Check that your local council will allow this.)

Preventing digging:
- Make sure your dog has plenty of interactive play every day, as well as lots of exercise.
- Redirect digging behaviour to another, more acceptable play.
- Give bones in a confined area where it is impossible for the dog to bury them.

House soiling

This is most common in puppies while they are being house-trained. House soiling may also occur in older dogs for various reasons.

firmly and give it one of its own toys to chew. Whenever you see it chewing its own toys, praise it.

If the puppy persists, try using a water pistol. Squirt the puppy in the face when it starts to chew. Do not say anything. It is best that the puppy associate the unpleasant event with the object it is chewing, not with you.

Water pistols can work with older dogs too. Another option is to apply a deterrent such as bitter lime to objects that may be chewed.

Preventing destructive behaviour:
- Train your young puppy to chew its own toys.
- Do not leave puppies or newly acquired older dogs alone with access to valuable furniture. Leave them in a laundry area with plenty of toys or maybe a bone to chew.

TOP: Destructive chewing is a nasty behavioural trait that is difficult to correct, as it often happens when a dog is left alone and there is no one around to intervene. It can become obsessive and very expensive.

If an adult dog suddenly starts house soiling, take it for a complete health check, as there may be an underlying problem such as cystitis (bladder infection) or enteritis (bowel infection). If the dog is old, there may be a problem with control of bladder or bowel, or it may be due to senility.

If the dog is house soiling only when the owners are out, it may be suffering from separation anxiety (see p76). This will require the help of an animal behaviourist. Other possible reasons include territorial marking and asserting dominance, or habit, as in dogs adopted from kennels.

Extreme excitement and overly submissive responses to people often trigger urination. This sometimes happens when owners return home or visitors arrive. The dog is apparently unaware that urine is being passed. Most will outgrow the excitement trigger as they gain better bladder control, and it is best ignored. Submissive urination, however, does require treatment.

If a male dog is lifting his leg inside, he may be marking out a territory and trying to assert his dominance over one or more people or other dogs in the household. This is sometimes seen if a new family member arrives, or someone comes to stay.

Neutering can achieve a 75 per cent reduction in this behaviour. Retraining may also be necessary. The offender should be confined to certain parts of the house and should always be under direct supervision when indoors. If he shows signs of marking, he should be startled with a foghorn or water pistol and put outside.

As with puppy training, it is important to take these dogs outside frequently and praise them for elimination. Male adult dogs will rarely void all their urine at one time so a long walk helps to encourage them to fully empty their bladders. This should also help to decrease the likelihood of marking indoors.

Dogs kept in groups indoors are most at risk for inappropriate elimination. Males and females may be stimulated to urine mark, and may also defecate indoors. It is easier to keep groups of dogs in an outdoor compound with minimal house access.

Dogs that have been kennelled all their lives, and are adopted at the end of their breeding life, commonly soil inside. They have learned to eliminate on hard surfaces, and the floor is no different to the base of a run or a concrete yard. These dogs need re-training and this is often difficult as substrate preference – getting used to eliminating on grass or earth as opposed to hard surfaces or carpet, is learned at a very young age (seven to eight weeks). Retraining is done in the same way as training a new puppy.

Particularly submissive dogs may urinate spontaneously when anyone reaches towards them. This is a normal canine response to meeting with a dominant animal, but can become quite a problem. Some of these dogs will assume a submissive posture and urinate simply because someone looks directly at them.

It is possible to train these dogs out of the behaviour by rewarding them for less submissive behaviour such as sitting and looking at their owners. Any rolling over or urinating should be ignored.

Preventing house soiling:
○ Train young puppies thoroughly.
○ Ensure adequate exercise and outdoor access especially for entire (non-neutered) males.

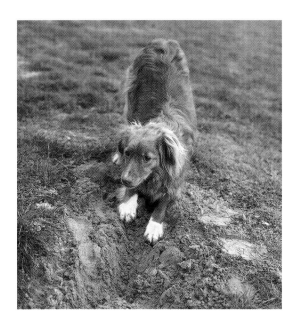

ABOVE: Although it is perfectly normal for a dog to dig holes, its owners are less likely to approve, especially if they also happen to be keen gardeners.

These dogs are extremely anxious when left alone. They require specialist treatment which usually involves anti-anxiety medication and a behaviour modification programme. This is a series of exercises that the dogs and owners must perform daily to teach the dogs to relax and to stay relaxed while their owners leave the room, and eventually the house.

Preventing separation anxiety:

- Make sure your puppy gets used to spending time alone.
- Try to avoid having the puppy spend time with one family member exclusively. Make sure it learns to feel comfortable with everyone.
- Avoid establishing a departure ritual. Vary the order of shower and breakfast. Put on shoes and coat then sit down for a cup of coffee.
- Don't make an issue out of leaving and don't fuss too much when you return.
- Exercise your dog well before leaving it alone for any length of time.

- Take time to make the dog feel at ease with newcomers.
- Keep groups of dogs in outdoor compounds.

Separation anxiety

Separation anxiety is a name used to describe the behaviour seen in some dogs when they are left alone, or when they are separated from one particular family member.

These dogs typically begin barking as soon as their owners leave and continue throughout their absence. They may chew doors, rip up carpet and curtains, destroy furniture and defecate and urinate inside. In extreme cases they have been known to jump through glass windows.

There may be an inherited predisposition to this condition. It is interesting that there is a high incidence of separation anxiety in dogs from animal shelters. It is unclear whether the condition is related to the trauma of being abandoned or if they were abandoned because owners could not cope with their separation anxiety.

TOP: Your dog depends on you, the leader of the pack, for comfort, companionship and food. Most dogs will learn to come to terms with their owner's absence during the day. In rare cases, separation anxiety may develop.

Obsessive compulsive disorder (OCD)

This is usually a normal behavioural trait that is being performed with abnormal frequency, to the point that it interferes with daily living and becomes a nuisance. Examples of this unacceptable behaviour include digging, chasing shadows, chasing their tails, snapping at imaginary flies, running along fence lines and chewing at feet.

Dogs with OCD cannot usually be distracted from their behaviour. If they are successfully enticed to stop, it is only for a short while and they soon return to it. Some dogs may become aggressive towards anyone who tries to physically prevent the behaviour from continuing, while others will not even stop long enough to go for a walk or eat properly. In very severe cases, such animals may damage themselves physically. Compulsive diggers may dig until their feet bleed and their nails are broken. Chewers and tail chasers may cause self-inflicted skin lesions and suffer secondary infections.

It seems that this condition may be inherited so it is wise not to breed from affected animals. Predisposed breeds include Scottish Terriers, Bull Terriers (tail chasing), and King Charles Spaniels (fly snapping).

Animals with OCD have a deficiency of certain neurochemicals in the brain, and need professional help. They require medication and behaviour modification designed to redirect their attention and to encourage relaxation. In many cases they need medication throughout life.

Preventing OCD: It is probably impossible to prevent this in genetically predisposed individuals.

Escaping

Some dogs insist on trying to escape and go exploring. This can be frustrating for owners and dangerous for the dogs.

If you own an escape artist, the single most important consideration is perimeter fencing. Ensure that this is at least 2–3m (6–10ft) high, or if the dog is likely to dig out, bury part of the fence 1m (3ft) below the ground. You could also use a sonic barrier, which emits a pulse of high-frequency sound at regular intervals. Another option is to build a secure pen with a concrete floor and a roof, in which you can leave the dog while you are out or too busy to interact with it.

It is important that your dog receives plenty of exercise and interactive play with you every day. If being involved in whatever you are doing stimulates your pet, it is less likely to wander off exploring. If your dog is well exercised it will probably be happy to relax and sleep while you are busy doing something boring, or if it has to stay home alone for a while.

Male dogs may run off after bitches in heat. Castration (see p37, Neutering) will deal with this problem.

ABOVE AND OPPOSITE: Although it looks comical when a dog chases its tail, this 'game' may become an obsession, especially in dogs that are frequently lonely.

PROTECTING YOUR DOG'S HEALTH
The veterinary clinic

To keep fit and well your dog needs regular health care. Some of it will be provided by you, and some by your local veterinary clinic or animal hospital.

Veterinary clinics are not just centres for the treatment of ill health. They are also a valuable source of practical information and friendly advice from veterinarians and their trained staff.

Most veterinary clinics also act as valuable community resource centres, providing information about local boarding facilities, dog groomers or dog-sitting services, for example. Many also have notice boards on which their clients can post information.

The changes in veterinary science over the years, and particularly during the last decade, have been remarkable. In addition to radiography (X-rays) and routine blood sampling, modern diagnostic aids include ultrasonography (the use of ultrasound scanning equipment), Magnetic Resonance Imaging (MRI) and Computer Assisted Tomography (CAT) scans. Other areas of veterinary specialisation include:

o Anaesthesia
o Orthopaedics
o Ophthalmology
o Endocrinology
o Dermatology

o Animal Behaviour
o Dentistry
o Medicine
o Surgery
o Radiology
o Diagnostic imaging

Certain methods of diagnosis and therapy – some ancient, some new – are now also becoming a recognised part of a comprehensive approach to animal health care. Known as Complementary Veterinary Medicine (or Complementary and Alternative Medicine – CAVM), many of these methods have been used in human medicine for years, but their integration into veterinary practice has been comparatively recent.

For example, some veterinarians are now trained in veterinary acupuncture and acutherapy (the examination and stimulation of specific points on the body of animals using acupuncture needles, injections, low-level lasers, magnets and a variety of other techniques for diagnosis and treatment), veterinary chiropractic (the examination, diagnosis and treatment through manipulation and adjustments of specific joints, particularly the vertebrae, and of areas of the skull), veterinary massage therapy, homeopathy, botanical medicine, nutritional therapy and even the use of flower essences (dilute extracts from certain flowers).

TOP: A simple Elizabethan collar, made from paper or sturdy plastic, will prevent a dog from scratching, licking or aggravating its wounds and causing secondary infection.

The immune system

The bodies of animals, like those of humans, have many defence mechanisms to protect them against the micro-organisms in the environment.

Primary barriers

o   Healthy skin acts as a physical barrier.
o   Mucous membranes in the nose, trachea and bronchi help to trap foreign substances and prevent them from entering the lungs.
o   Acid in the stomach kills many invading organisms.
o   Mucus produced from the lining of the intestines acts as a barrier.
o   The liver destroys toxins produced by bacteria.
o   Organisms are excreted in faeces and urine.

These defence mechanisms work well when an animal is healthy, but are less effective if it is weakened, unhealthy or mentally or physically stressed.

Most organisms that cause disease consist mainly of proteins. If an organism gets past the primary barriers, the body quickly detects its 'foreign' proteins and produces antibodies against them. Antibodies are produced by specialised white blood cells found mainly in the lymph nodes and spleen. They circulate in the blood and are usually very specific, destroying only the organism (the antigen) that stimulated their production.

The first time the dog's body encounters a disease, introduced from the environment or by means of a vaccine, it may take up to 10 days to produce antibodies. The next time the disease is encountered, antibody production occurs rapidly, preventing the disease from becoming established.

ABOVE: Some dogs may develop a real fear of the veterinary clinic: if this happens, visit your clinic socially and ask your vet and clinic technician to fuss over the dog and give it treats.

Antibody levels wane with time, but if the antigen is encountered again (either through infection or a booster vaccination), antibody production immediately resumes. Immunity created by vaccines is not generally as long lasting as the 'natural immunity' created by exposure to a disease. This explains why booster vaccinations may be needed to keep an animal protected.

Passive (maternal) immunity

Passive immunity occurs when a newborn animal acquires antibodies from its mother.

Newborn animals have a rudimentary immune system that takes six to 12 weeks to fully develop. To tide them over this period they receive passive immunity from their mother in the form of antibodies, some of which enter their body while they are still in the uterus, but most of which are taken in with the mother's colostrum (first milk). This is a critical period for the newborn animal, as it can only absorb these antibodies during the first day or two after birth. If a bitch has a prolonged whelping or gives birth to a large litter, the early puppies will have more opportunity to ingest colostrum than those born later, so the degree of passive immunity may vary between littermates.

A bitch can only pass on antibodies to the diseases that she herself has encountered, or against which she has been vaccinated. A bitch that is not vaccinated, or lives in isolation from other dogs, will have fewer antibodies to pass on, and her puppies will be more vulnerable from birth. A bitch

TOP AND OPPOSITE: Vaccinations can be given either under the skin or as drops into the nostrils of a dog. Your vet will advise you which type of vaccination is necessary for your pet.

used for breeding must be vaccinated, and her booster vaccinations should be kept up to date.

Passive immunity is temporary: the amount of antibodies in the blood halve every seven days or so, and after three months it has almost disappeared.

Active immunity

Active immunity is the result of an animal producing antibodies from its own immune system, in response to disease or vaccination.

To be protected, puppies must develop their own, active immunity, by contact with a disease or through vaccination.

While passive immunity is high the puppy is protected from disease, and its own immune system may not respond to a vaccination. However, some brands of vaccine are designed to over-ride passive immunity and stimulate the puppy's immune system.

Some puppies may lose passive immunity before three months, so these puppies will be at risk if they are not vaccinated and are exposed to a virus.

The typical recommendation for a puppy from a bitch that has been properly vaccinated is to receive two vaccinations, one at nine weeks of age and the other at three months. In areas of high risk, vaccination may be started at six weeks and repeated at fortnightly intervals until three months. Ask your veterinarian for advice about the situation in your area.

Vaccinating your dog

While still with the breeder, some six-week-old puppies will have received a temporary vaccination against distemper, hepatitis and canine parvovirus. At nine weeks your puppy should be vaccinated against canine distemper, infectious canine hepatitis (ICH), canine parvovirus (CPV) and 'kennel cough'. Depending on where you live, it may also

need vaccinations for other diseases such as leptospirosis or rabies. A booster will be required three weeks later.

Many different brands of vaccine are available. Some are effective against several diseases, which reduces the number of injections required. Your veterinarian will advise you which vaccines are the most suitable for your dog.

Canine distemper

This is the first virus disease of dogs for which a vaccine was specifically developed. The distemper virus also affects ferrets, foxes, skinks, raccoons and wolves. Once a killer disease, it is now uncommon in many countries because of long-term routine vaccination programmes. Originally it was most often seen in young animals, although now adult dogs are likely to be affected. This is usually because their vaccinations have not been kept up to date.

Early symptoms include loss of appetite, and affected dogs develop a respiratory infection accompanied by a sore throat, coughing and fever and a thick yellow purulent discharge from the eyes and nose. There may be enteritis accompanied by diarrhoea.

In some dogs the disease progresses during the next two to three weeks, as the virus infects the nervous system, causing muscle tremors, seizures and even

BY BREATHING AIRBORNE VIRUSES

THROUGH DIRECT CONTACT

BY EATING CONTAMINATED FOODS

FROM INSECT OR ANIMAL BITES

BY DIRECT CONTACT THROUGH
OPEN CUTS OR WOUNDS

BY DRINKING CONTAMINATED
MOTHER'S MILK

As viruses can be transmitted in a number of ways, it is not always easy to tell how a dog may have contracted a viral disease

paralysis. Dogs that recover may be left with permanent damage to their nervous system, and those infected as puppies often show deformities of the enamel on their permanent teeth caused by damage while these were growing. Some dogs develop thickened pads, hence distemper's other name: 'hard pad' disease.

Canine parvovirus (CPV) infection

This disease is similar to feline enteritis in cats, and may have resulted from a mutation in that cat virus. It first appeared in the late 1970s and spread rapidly around the world. It is spread by dog-to-dog contact through the faeces, and the virus is easily carried from one place to another on the hair or feet of infected dogs, on contaminated cages and on human clothing or footwear. The virus can survive for long periods, and is resistant to extremes in environmental conditions.

In very young puppies this disease causes inflammation of the heart muscle (myocarditis), often resulting in sudden death and a very high death rate among litters. Puppies that survive can take weeks to recover. In older puppies and adults it causes fever, enteritis (accompanied by diarrhoea and vomiting) and a death rate of up to 10 per cent.

Infectious canine hepatitis (ICH)

This virus infection occurs mainly in young dogs, is highly infectious and can cause serious liver damage. Many infected dogs show no symptoms, while others may simply appear 'off-colour' over a long period of time. In both cases these dogs excrete the virus in their urine and spread the infection amongst other dogs.

Symptoms can vary from a mild fever to a serious illness, followed by death within a few hours. Affected dogs lose their appetite, are very thirsty, have a discharge from the eyes and nose and may develop bloody diarrhoea. Early treatment of affected animals is essential if there is to be any hope of recovery. Some that survive develop opacity of the cornea of the eye, which makes it appear blue.

Kennel cough

This mild, self-limiting disease can affect dogs at any age, and is caused by a combination of various infectious agents, including the bacterium *Bordetella bronchiseptica* and canine parainfluenza virus. Inflammation in the trachea and bronchi causes varying degrees of 'dry' cough, sometimes accompanied by retching or gagging.

Kennel cough is a highly contagious disease and is transmitted through moisture droplets coughed into the air by affected animals; this is why it spreads rapidly among dogs that are closely confined, such as in kennels (hence the name given to the disease), hospitals and pet stores. The peak time for infection is during the summer months when dogs are more likely to be brought together in boarding kennels. Kennel cough is more of a nuisance than a threat to life, but the dry cough can persist for up to three weeks, causing the dog (and its owner as well) a great deal of distress. Kennel cough often gets worse when the dog is excited.

Vaccines are available, given every three months by injection under the skin or by placing drops directly into the dog's nose.

Most boarding kennels will not accept dogs unless they have been recently vaccinated.

Leptospirosis

This is another disease against which dogs should be routinely vaccinated. There are many different types (serovars) of *Leptospira* bacteria, all of which are spread through infected urine. The bacteria can also infect humans. Symptoms of infection depend on the serovar involved. For example, *Leptospira canicola* infects the kidneys and frequently results in chronic kidney disease. In mild cases the dog may merely appear 'off-colour' for a few days. In serious cases, signs include lethargy, bad breath (caused by uraemia, the accumulation of urea in the blood), ulceration in the mouth, and vomiting. In advanced cases there is severe abdominal pain. Treatment includes antibiotics and therapy to replace lost fluids. Recovered dogs have kidney damage that contributes to chronic kidney disease later in life.

Leptospira icterohaemorrhagiae, often caught from rats, infects the liver and causes substantial damage. In acute cases death can occur quickly. Signs include lethargy,

vomiting, bloody diarrhoea and jaundice. Early treatment with antibiotics and fluid replacement is essential.

Rabies

In countries, such as Canada, where this viral disease is endemic, dogs are routinely protected by vaccination. Rabies can affect any mammal and is almost always fatal. Transmitted through the saliva of infected animals, usually the result of a bite, it can also be spread by infected saliva coming into contact with mucous membranes (eye, nose or mouth) or a skin wound.

In Europe, foxes are the main carriers of the infection; in Mexico and other Latin and Central American countries, the culprits are dogs. In Canada and the United States, the most common carriers – foxes, skunks, bats, raccoons and coyotes – often live close to people. This proximity poses a continuing threat of infection for farm animals, pets and people.

The incubation period can range from two weeks to six months. In its early stages, rabies commonly causes behaviour and personality changes – for example, nocturnal animals are seen out during the day, wild animals may lose their fear of humans, and quiet animals may become excitable or even turn aggressive. Affected dogs tend to hide away from light.

As the disease progresses, about 25 per cent of affected dogs show the 'furious' form and are likely to attack without provocation. Animals affected by the 'furious' form of rabies are extremely dangerous. Within six days of the appearance of their symptoms they usually enter a coma and die.

The remainder develop the 'dumb' form, in which early paralysis of the throat and cheek muscles make it unable to

Human health and Leptospirosis

Leptospirosis is only one of several dog diseases that can infect humans. Always be aware of the need for hygiene. Make sure all family members (especially children) wash their hands after handling a dog. If you need to handle a dog that may be infected with leptospirosis, wear rubber gloves.

ABOVE: In this microscopic view of a dog's brain, the small red bodies inside the purple brain cells are indicative of a rabies infection.

swallow, so that saliva drools from its mouth. These animals rarely survive more than two weeks.

Prevention: Because most of Canada's rabies is carried by wildlife, control is particularly difficult. Dropping vaccinated baits from the air; hand-baiting urban habitats; trapping, vaccinating and then releasing raccoons; and regular pet vaccinations are among measures used to contain the disease. Anyone bringing a dog across the US border into Canada has to provide proof of vaccination against rabies in the previous 36 months: rabies tags alone are not sufficient. Proof of vaccination is also required for animals travelling from Canada to the United States.

Anyone planning to take a pet overseas should check with the host country. Many island nations in which the disease is not endemic (such as Hawaii, Australia and New Zealand) have strict quarantine laws to prevent its introduction. In Britain the PETS scheme allows vaccinated cats and dogs to enter under certain conditions. Canadian pets do not conform to those conditions and so would be quarantined before entering Britain.

Precautions: If your dog fights with any mammal that is a rabies carrier, saliva carrying the virus could be present on its coat or in any of its wounds. Take these precautions:

○ Do not try to capture the attacking animal.
○ Use gloves and a towel when handling your pet.
○ Call Animal Control or an equivalent organisation.
○ Take your pet to a veterinarian.
○ If your pet has a current rabies vaccination, get advice about giving a booster within 72 hours.

If you are bitten or scratched by an animal suspected of being rabid, or if saliva from the animal enters an open wound or comes into contact with your nose, eyes or mouth, wash the wound or contact area with household detergent or soap. These kill the virus faster than any disinfectant. It is essential that you then get

medical attention immediately. The treatment involves a course of vaccinations.

Routine rabies prevention:

○ Make sure your pet has a rabies shot every year.
○ Do not let your pets run free, especially at night.
○ Do not touch or play with animals you do not know.
○ Do not touch animals that look sick, even if you want to help them. Do not pick up dead or abandoned animals.
○ Do not feed or attract wildlife into your garden, and do not try to capture wildlife.
○ Get rid of any bats inhabiting barns or cottage attics.
○ Report all biting incidents to your local health unit
○ Call your local rabies control hotline or health unit if you see a dead suspect rabid animal.

Parasites

Dogs may suffer from a variety of parasites, which are grouped into internal parasites (those that live within the body, such as worms) and external parasites (those that live

TOP LEFT AND RIGHT: This stray, eight-week old mixed-breed puppy arrived in its new home with a severe case of roundworm. After six weeks and the correct treatment, it is altogether a different creature.

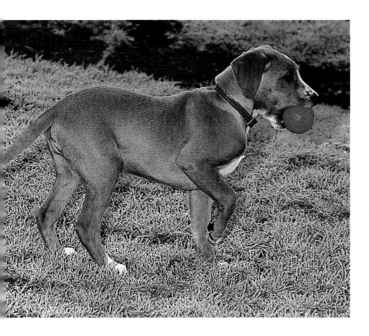

on or in the skin, such as fleas and mites). Most parasites are host-specific, which means that they infect one particular species of animal only. Among the exceptions, though, are the cat flea, cattle tick and sheep tick, which may also infect dogs.

Worms

A variety of worm species can infect dogs. These are classified according to their shape or the region of the body that they infect. Those of most importance in the dog – and therefore to their human owner – are roundworms, hookworms, whipworms, tapeworms, lungworms and heartworms.

Roundworms: The two most common species found in dogs, *Toxocara canis* and *Toxascaris leonina*, are ascarid worms.

Toxocara canis is particularly important because of its ability to infect puppies before they are born. An infected bitch has

roundworm larvae lying dormant in her muscles and other tissues, and these are largely unaffected by many routine worm treatments. Hormones released during pregnancy stimulate these larvae to migrate; some move into the bitch's intestine and develop into adult worms, others migrate into her uterus and into the unborn puppies' lungs. At birth, more larvae are excreted in the bitch's milk.

The result is that almost every puppy is born with a roundworm infection, and all are likely to be infected as soon as they suckle. During the next few days and weeks they will also pick up infection by ingesting some of the roundworm eggs now being produced by adult worms in the bitch's intestine and passed out in her faeces.

In an infected puppy the larvae migrate through the intestinal wall and, via the liver, to the lungs. If there is a large number of larvae, the puppy may cough and have breathing problems – it may even develop pneumonia.

From the lungs some larvae enter the bloodstream and are circulated to the muscles and other tissues, where they form cysts and lie dormant. Others are coughed up and swallowed. By the time the puppy is two weeks old these have developed into adult worms capable of laying thousands of eggs. Some adult worms may be clearly visible in the puppy's faeces – these then infect the bitch when she licks the puppy clean.

ABOVE: The correct way to administer tablets to a dog is to press its upper lips over its upper teeth and firmly force the muzzle open. Use your other hand to place the tablet as far back on the tongue as possible. Hold the muzzle closed and the dog's head back until the tablet is swallowed.

LARVAE CAN BE SWALLOWED

LARVAE DEVELOP IN
DIGESTIVE SYSTEM

2 000 EGGS PASS
THROUGH DAILY

TRANSPORTED BY MICE

DOGS AND CATS
INGEST EGGS BY
EATING GRASS

EGGS ARE ABLE TO LIE
DORMANT IN THE SOIL
FOR YEARS

MOTHER'S MILK

TRANSFERRED TO HUMANS

LARVAE GROW IN 2 TO 4 WEEKS

FAECES ARE A MAIN SOURCE OF INFECTION

The life cycle of the roundworm and its interaction with its hosts and humans

Puppies suffering from a heavy roundworm infestation have a harsh coat, fail to grow properly and suffer from diarrhoea and a visibly bloated abdomen. If worms are present in sufficiently large numbers they can physically block the stomach and intestines.

Toxocara canis can also have an 'indirect' life cycle, in which infective larvae lodge in the tissues of another animal such as a rabbit (called a paratenic host), and only develop further if that animal is eaten by a dog.

Infection with *Toxascaris leonina* is less of a problem because its larvae do not migrate through the lungs and body tissues, but complete their development within the walls of the bitch's intestine. Therefore puppies do not become infected with this particular roundworm before birth or through drinking the bitch's milk, or suffer from its larvae migrating through their lungs and other body tissues.

Treatment: Assume that, to some degree, all nursing bitches and their puppies are infected with roundworms, so start treatment as soon as possible. Some vets recommend that a pregnant bitch be treated every two weeks; others suggest less often. Discuss the situation with your vet.

At the time of writing, there is unfortunately no product that will remove all encysted or migrating roundworm larvae, so treatment aims at destroying any developing adult worms in the intestine.

The first worm treatment for puppies is usually given when they are two to three weeks old, followed by further treatments every one to two weeks until they are three months old. Further worming should be given at monthly intervals until six months, and then three or four times a year for the rest of each dog's life. Your veterinary clinic will recommend products and a regime appropriate to your area.

Because of the hazard to human health, everyone, especially children, must thoroughly wash their hands after handling young puppies.

Make sure you properly dispose of faeces from a nursing bitch and her puppies. Burn them in the garden, or flush them down the toilet. Do not bury or compost them, because under the right conditions roundworm eggs can survive for years.

Hookworms

These small, round-bodied, blood-sucking worms live in the dog's intestine and, if present in sufficient numbers, can cause severe anaemia and death.

The two species most commonly encountered in dogs are *Ancylostoma caninum* and *Uncinaria stenocephala*. In some areas another species, *A. braziliensis*, also occurs. The most common hookworm in tropical and subtropical areas is

Worms and the human

The eggs from roundworms and hookworms can infect humans. Puppies (and kittens) are often infected with worms, and children are especially at risk, particularly those at the thumb-sucking stage.

Dogs (adults and puppies) that are harbouring worms shed worm eggs in their faeces, and under the right conditions these can remain for years in grass or soil in home gardens and community parks.

When swallowed by a human, roundworm eggs hatch into infective larvae that do not develop into adult worms but wander through the body, causing damage. They are potentially dangerous because they move through internal body tissues (a process called *visceral larva migrans*). The disease is called toxocariasis, and it produces a variety of symptoms depending on which tissues are affected. Occasionally larvae become encysted in the retina at the back of the eye, causing partial loss of sight or even total blindness.

Proper hygiene is essential. Make sure that children and all members of the family wash their hands after handling or playing with a dog, and before they eat. Do not allow a dog to lick somebody's face, or to eat off crockery used by humans.

If hookworms infect humans, the larvae enter and migrate through the skin, leaving a visible raised, irregular track (a process called *cutaneous larva migrans*). The disease is self-limiting and a spontaneous cure occurs after several weeks.

Two dog tapeworms, the hydatid tapeworm (*Echinococcus granulosus*) and the flea tapeworm (*Dipylidium caninum*), can infect humans. The flea tapeworm rarely causes problems, but the hydatid tapeworm is potentially lethal, causing hydatid disease. Cysts develop in the liver and lungs, and less commonly the heart, kidneys and central nervous system, and death can result. Children are commonly infected, but because the cysts are slow growing it can be many years before the disease is recognised.

Dog and cat fleas (*Ctenocephalides canis* and *Ctenocephalides felis*) bite humans. Most people suffer no more than minor irritation, but some are allergic to fleas and may develop a more serious skin reaction. Proper flea control will minimise the problem.

A. caninum, whereas in the United Kingdom, Europe, Canada and northern United States, *Uncinaria stenocephala* is more likely to be implicated.

Adult hookworms lay eggs that are passed out with the faeces and hatch into larvae on the ground. Under the right conditions (damp and humid soil) these can survive for many months. In places where dogs congregate and defecate, such as public parks where faeces have not been removed, or grass runs in breeding or boarding kennels with poor hygiene, large numbers of infective larvae can build up.

Dogs become infected either by swallowing larvae or by penetration of larvae through the skin; the most common site of penetration is between the toes, and this often causes itching and dermatitis. Larvae eventually reach the dog's intestine and develop into adult worms to complete the cycle.

Hookworm larvae can also penetrate human skin.

Ancylostoma caninum larvae can infect puppies via the bitch's milk in a similar way to *Toxacara canis*. When any dog becomes infected, some larvae migrate through body tissues and become encysted in the muscles, where they lie dormant. In a bitch, hormonal changes in late pregnancy stimulate the encysted larvae to migrate into her mammary glands. They are then ingested by the puppies when they drink the colostrum, and later the milk.

The symptoms of hookworm infection include poor growth in puppies or loss of condition in adults, diarrhoea and anaemia. Treatment is the same as for roundworms.

Whipworms

Trichuris vulpis has a 'direct' life cycle in which eggs laid by adult worms in the intestine are passed out in the faeces and hatch out into infective larvae that are then capable of infecting a dog and growing into adult worms.

Symptoms of whipworm infection include failure to gain weight or loss of condition, diarrhoea and, in severe infestations, anaemia.

Tapeworms

Tapeworms have an 'indirect' life cycle in which another animal (called the intermediate host) must eat the worm eggs before the larvae inside them can develop any further. When a dog eats the intermediate host, the cycle is completed and the adult worm develops.

Several species of tapeworm can infect dogs: *Taenia taeniaeformis*, *Taenia pisiformis*, *Taenia hydatigena* and *Taenia ovis*. Although some of these worms can grow to up to 3m (10ft) long, they usually cause few health problems and often go unnoticed.

One of the more common tapeworms is *Dipylidium caninum*, often called the 'flea tapeworm' because fleas act as the intermediate host. One of the first signs of tapeworm

1 DOG EATS CONTAMINATED OFFAL

2 SEGMENTS DEPOSITED IN FAECES

4 VEGETATION CONTAMINATED

5 INTERMEDIATE HOSTS CAN BE SHEEP, RABBITS, RODENTS OR HUMANS

3 INFECTED HUMANS CAN DEVELOP DANGEROUS HYDATID CYSTS

The life cycle of the hydatid tapeworm

TOP: The whipworm hatches from its egg, within the dog's body.

infection is the presence of tapeworm segments sticking to the hair around a dog's anus, lying on its bedding or in its faeces. Initially these resemble cucumber seeds, but when dry they look more like grains of rice.

From the time your puppy is three months old, treat it monthly against tapeworms and roundworms until it is six months old. Thereafter, worm every three months throughout your dog's life. Many worm preparations are only effective against particular parasites, so obtain advice from your veterinary clinic as to which to use. Proper flea control will help to reduce the incidence of *Dipylidium caninum*.

The hydatid tapeworm, *Echinococcus granulosus*, is particularly serious because it poses a risk to human health.

The worm itself is only about 7mm (0.2in) long, but an infected dog may harbour more than a thousand. Eggs passed out in the dog's faeces are eaten by a variety of intermediate hosts, among which are sheep and humans. Inside the intermediate host, the eggs develop into larvae that form cysts in the tissues, especially the liver and lungs.

Working dogs on farms, especially sheep farms, are the most at risk because they may have access to raw offal containing the cysts.

In some countries where *Echinococcus* infection was proving a problem, for example Wales and New Zealand, national control schemes were introduced that prohibited the feeding of raw offal to dogs and ensured that all working dogs were wormed regularly.

Lungworms

Lungworms (*Filaroides osleri*) also have a 'direct' life cycle. Adult worms develop in small (2mm; 0.8in) nodules in an infected dog's trachea and bronchi. They lay eggs that are coughed up, and either swallowed and passed out in the faeces, or transmitted through the dog's saliva. A mild infection of lungworms in a dog may go unnoticed. In more severe infections, though, symptoms include weight loss and a protracted, harsh cough, especially during even moderate exercise.

Treatment of lungworms can sometimes prove difficult, although today there are several different drugs available. Ask your vet for advice.

Heartworms

The heartworm (*Dirofilaria immitis*) infection is spread directly from dog to dog by certain species of biting mosquito. Heartworm larvae (called microfilariae) circulate in the blood of an infected dog. When a mosquito sucks blood from that dog it also ingests the microfilariae, transferring them to other dogs that it bites. After the microfilariae enter the bloodstream, they travel in the circulation to the heart, lungs and large blood vessels, where they eventually mature into adults that begin to produce the next generation of microfilariae. After being bitten by an infected mosquito it may be six to seven months before microfilariae can be detected in a dog's blood, so heartworm disease is not often confirmed in dogs under a year old.

In the early stages of heartworm infection a dog will show few symptoms, but these develop later as large numbers of parasites become established and cause damage to the lining of the heart and obstruct the heart and blood circulation.

An affected dog gradually loses weight, becomes lethargic and starts to tire easily. It may develop a persistent cough and become anaemic and pot-bellied. Eventually it may suffer right-sided heart failure.

If you live in an area where heartworm disease occurs, your dog may need regular blood tests to determine whether it is infected. Talk to your veterinarian about this.

Tests include microscopic examination of a blood sample from your dog to detect the microfilariae, using a special stain to make them more visible. At least half of all infected dogs have no circulating microfilariae, so you may find that other tests are needed to help confirm the presence of the disease.

5

THE MICROFILARIA GROW TO ADULT STAGE INSIDE THE HEART

1

ADULT HEARTWORM LAYS ITS YOUNG

4

2–3 MONTHS LATER, THE MICRO-FILARIA MOVE TO THE DOG'S HEART

3

THE MOSQUITO BITES OTHER DOGS AND INFECTS THEM

2

MOSQUITO BITES THE DOG AND IS INFECTED WITH MICROFILARIA

The life cycle of the heartworm: this worm is unique in that it is spread from dog to dog by certain species of biting mosquito

Uninfected dogs can be given a course of drugs to prevent infection, and infected dogs can be treated. Treatment sometimes results in severe side effects because dead worms disintegrate in the bloodstream and cause blockages in some blood vessels.

Protozoan infections

Toxoplasmosis

Toxoplasmosis, caused by the protozoan parasite *Toxoplasma gondii*, is common in cats and can be spread to humans from the ingestion of the cysts passed out in cat faeces. Toxoplasma infections in dogs are uncommon and most go unnoticed, but dog owners should be aware that a dog that eats cat faeces can become infected and may suffer similar symptoms to infected humans.

Humans can become infected through:

○ handling contaminated cat litter or garden soil in which cats have defaecated

○ accidentally ingesting contaminated soil on unwashed fruit or vegetables

○ eating raw or undercooked meat (especially sheep meat)

○ consuming unpasteurised goat's milk, yoghurt or cheese.

One in two humans have a chance of becoming infected at some stage of their life. Initial infection may pass unnoticed or cause little more than 'flu-like symptoms.

However, the parasite may become encysted in various tissues, causing inflammation, and toxoplasmosis is especially dangerous to pregnant women, in whom it may cause abortion or infect the baby in the womb. An infected baby may be born blind or retarded.

As a routine precaution, cat faeces should be removed from a litter tray every two days, before any toxoplasma eggs in them become infective.

Coccidiosis

Four species of coccidia (*Cystoisospora*) can infect dogs, although their occurrence is uncommon. Young puppies are most at risk, and symptoms include diarrhoea, dehydration and weight loss. Diagnosis is by laboratory examination of faecal samples. Veterinary treatment is essential.

Giardiasis

The protozoan parasite *Giardia lamblia* occurs worldwide and can infect humans, most domestic animals and birds. Adults (trophozoites) mainly inhabit the mucosal surfaces of the small intestine, where they interfere with digestion. They produce cysts that are passed out in the faeces. These cysts often end up in water, which then becomes a source of infection. In pet animals, giardiasis is principally a problem of dogs, but cats are occasionally infected. Signs vary from mild to severe diarrhoea that may be persistent, intermittent or self-limiting. Some animals experience weight loss, others do not.

The disease is diagnosed by laboratory examination of faecal samples. There are several drugs that may be used for veterinary treatment.

Fleas

As soon as you get your puppy, treat it for fleas, even though it may not appear to be infested. Your vet will advise you about the best available treatments for these external parasites, which will need repeating throughout your dog's life. If you have a cat, make sure that you treat it as well, because the cat flea is the most common flea species found on dogs.

Permitted to go unchecked, fleas can transmit internal parasites; dogs eating adult fleas can become infected with the tapeworm *Dipylidium caninum*. Fleas themselves can also be carriers for diseases such as bubonic plague and endemic typhus.

The adult female flea feeds for two to three days, consuming up to 15 times her own body weight of blood every day, then begins to lay eggs. At peak production a female can lay up to 50 eggs a day, and many hundreds of eggs in her lifetime. The eggs are not attached, and normally drop off onto the floor, carpet, animal's bedding or ground.

The eggs hatch out into legless larvae that find their way into cracks where they feed on organic debris. This includes flakes of skin and the faeces of adult fleas (which contain incompletely digested blood). After four to eight days the larvae spin a protective cocoon and form pupae.

These flea pupae can remain dormant for up to two years and are particularly resistant to some of the most commonly used insecticides.

The flea pupae hatch when the environmental conditions are right – the hotter and more humid, the better.

Hatching is triggered by the warmth or vibrations of a potential host (dog, cat or human), and can take less than a second. Newly hatched fleas can leap about half a metre (20in), about 1,200 times their own body length, and move onto a host to feed. Under ideal conditions the complete cycle can take as little as three weeks.

Fleas spend quite a lot of time off the host and in the environment, so treatment must aim at two things:

○ killing adult fleas on the dog and in the surroundings
○ breaking the life cycle by killing eggs and larvae in the surroundings.

Treating the animal: Treating a dog for fleas will kill the adults on it and the few eggs that may remain in the dog's coat. There are many effective treatments available, some of which kill 95-100 per cent of fleas on dogs and cats in 12 hours. Applied to the skin, they spread over the skin

TOP: The adult flea, laying an egg. At peak production she could lay up to 50 eggs a day. The eggs drop off onto the carpet or the dog's bedding – or your bedding, if you're not careful.

surface and kill adults on contact. They also kill 99 per cent of flea larvae in the pet's immediate surroundings. The effects of such treatments last for about a month.

It is not enough just to treat your dog, though; you must treat any cats in the household, and treat the home environment as well.

Treating the environment: Because fleas spend only a short part of their life cycle on a dog, it is important to treat the immediate environment in which the adult fleas live, and where their eggs develop.

Regular vacuuming of carpets and special attention to crevices in wooden floors and along skirting boards will help to physically remove many of them, but it also concentrates larvae inside the vacuum bag, together with plenty of organic matter for them to continue feeding. If the bag is disposable, remove and burn it. If not, put a flea collar into it to kill the inhabitants.

Flea 'bombs' or 'foggers' are available to treat the home. These release an insecticidal mist containing permethrin, which kills adult fleas, and methoprene, an insect growth regulator based on a natural compound found in insects that prevents the development of flea larvae. It remains in the carpet for up to nine months and prevents eggs and larvae developing.

For the most effective results you should treat the whole house. Each of the rooms to be treated must be vacated and closed off, and any fish or house plants should be removed.

Once you have prepared the house, let off the bomb and close the rooms for at least two hours. Next, open the doors and windows to ensure that the rooms are properly ventilated before people and animals are allowed to re-enter, 30 minutes later. If you use one of these products, follow the instructions on the label.

Some carpet shampoos contain insecticides that will kill fleas, and regular use of these may help control the problem.

Flea-bite dermatitis: Many dogs (and cats) develop an allergy to flea saliva. In temperate climates it is often called 'summer eczema', and even one flea bite can trigger off a severe reaction that has the dog scratching and biting itself, causing damage to its skin. In many cases, veterinary treatment is essential, because the allergic reaction must be controlled. Any severe skin damage needs to be treated to prevent bacterial infection and promote healing.

Ticks

Ticks mainly infest farm livestock, particularly sheep and cattle, and certain wild animals. In temperate climates they are more active during the summer months.

Deer tick bites, resulting in Lyme Disease, have become a serious health threat to people and animals in parts of Canada. For dogs, the disease is easily prevented through yearly vaccinations.

ABOVE: Unfortunately, a far-too familiar sight: a dog scratching frantically at its fleas. It's not enough to treat only your dog – treat all your other household animals and your home.

If you live in a tick-infested area, or have taken your dog for a walk through countryside where livestock or deer have been grazing, thoroughly check your dog's skin to locate and remove any ticks.

Pay special attention to the inside of your dog's ears, head, neck and shoulders, between its forelegs and under its belly. Keep in mind, however, that once engorged with blood, some ticks drop off again. In some cases all that is visible is a rash around the bite site.

When removing a tick, try to extract the head, otherwise an abscess may form. This removal is not always easy to accomplish.

You could spray the tick with a flea spray, leave it for 12 hours, then remove the dead tick.

For a quicker result, though, you could dab some methylated spirits or alcohol onto the tick to relax or kill it, wait a few minutes, then use a pair of fine-pointed tweezers to grip the tick near its head and pull it out with a sharp jerk. Do not grip it by the body, though, because squeezing it could result in the injection of more saliva, which might contain toxin (see tick paralysis, below).

If an abscess forms at the site, bathe it in warm saline and use an antibacterial ointment recommended by your vet.

Tick paralysis: Many ticks do no more than cause temporary discomfort, but in warm coastal areas of Australia there is an *Ixodes* species whose saliva contains a toxin that can cause gradual paralysis and even death. Symptoms of tick paralysis develop about four to five days after the tick infestation of your dog.

Initially, affected dogs show weakness in the hindquarters. This extends forwards, and there may be some change in the tone of the bark and some difficulty in breathing. Eventually paralysis may lead to death from respiratory failure. Veterinary treatment is essential.

Lice

These are uncommon, and are usually found on neglected dogs. There are several types, of which the most common is the biting louse (*Trichodectes canis*), which chews on flakes of skin and causes mild irritation. A more severe irritation is caused by the common sucking louse (*Linognathus setosus*), which penetrates the skin to feed on tissue fluids and blood, and can cause anaemia.

Louse eggs (nits) can be seen attached to hairs. The tiny grey-white adult lice, about 2mm (0.08in) long, can be seen particularly around the ears, head, neck, shoulders and anus.

Because lice spend the whole of their life cycle on their host, treatment is easy and consists of insecticide sprays or washes given at five- to seven-day intervals for at least three treatments. Infected bedding should be destroyed and the area disinfected.

Ear mites

There are several species of mite that an infect dogs.

Ear mites (*Otodectes cynotis*) usually cause most problems for puppies, but also infect adult dogs and cats. They cause irritation that leads to the dog scratching and the introduction of a secondary bacterial infection that causes inflammation and pain. Diagnosis is by microscopic examination of a swab taken from the ear.

Uncomplicated cases of ear mite infection may be treated with insecticidal ear drops (if you own a cat, treat it as well). If secondary infection is present, though, antibiotic treatment (with drops and/or by injection) will be necessary.

Mange mites

Three species of mange mite most commonly infect dogs.

Cheyletiella yasguri lives among the hairs and on the skin surface and causes scaling (dandruff) and irritation, which may lead to hair loss and skin infection.

ABOVE: When you remove a tick from your dog, try to extract the head, otherwise an abscess may form.

The sarcoptic mange mite (*Sarcoptes scabei*) and the demodectic mange mite (*Demodex canis*) can cause severe problems in dogs.

Demodectic mites enter the hair follicles, causing hair loss and mild irritation.

Sarcoptic mites burrow into the skin and cause severe irritation, which sets the animal rubbing, scratching and biting. Symptoms include itchiness and the appearance of bare patches where hair has been rubbed off or fallen out. Veterinary diagnosis is by microscopic examination of skin scrapings.

Treatment of C*heyletiella* infestation is fairly simple, using an insecticide lotion or cream. Treatment of sarcoptic or demodectic mange is more difficult and prolonged because the mites burrow deep within the skin.

1 TIE A SOFT BANDAGE AROUND THE MUZZLE.

2 TAKE THE CLOTH AROUND THE NECK AND TIE AT THE BACK.

Temporary muzzles can be made from soft belts, ties or even old tights

Harvest mites (chiggers)

These small mites (*Trombicula autumnalis*) occur in some areas. As their name implies, they are most common in late summer/early autumn, during or after harvest time. The adult mites are free-living, but their small red larvae are parasitic. In dogs these larvae, just visible to the naked eye, most commonly infect the feet between the toes (the interdigital spaces) and the small pocket at the lower edge of the ear flap. They cause irritation, and affected dogs constantly rub their ears and/or lick their feet. If your dog becomes infected, your veterinarian can recommend a suitable treatment.

ABOVE: The correct way to restrain a dog is to place it on a firm surface, put one arm gently around its neck and the other under its abdomen. Use both arms to hold the dog firmly against your body.

A basic first-aid kit

The information given here is for guidance only, and is not intended to replace veterinary advice. If faced with an emergency, remember that the principles of first aid for dogs are similar to those for humans.

- Rolls of 5cm (2in) and 7.5 (3in) bandage
- Self-adhesive bandage
- Roll of 5cm (2in) crepe bandage
- Roll of 5cm (2in) and 7.5 (3in) wide adhesive plaster
- Non-stick gauze pads
- Cotton wool balls
- Tweezers
- Curved, blunt-ended scissors
- Straight scissors
- Length of strong, soft bandage or tape to use as an emergency muzzle (see p94)

- Nail clipper
- Antiseptic and disinfectant liquids recommended by your vet
- Tube of antiseptic cream
- Hydrogen peroxide (3 per cent) for flushing wounds
- Mineral oil for treatment of constipation
- Ear and eye drops as recommended by your vet
- Roll of absorbent paper towel
- Leg from old pair of pantyhose (to put over the head if ears are bleeding)
- Old sock (to protect a dressing on the lower limb)

MONITORING YOUR DOG'S HEALTH
Signs of illness

The earlier you can detect a health problem in your dog and do something about it, the better. Treatment is more likely to be effective, and your dog will probably suffer less discomfort or pain. Learn what is normal, so you can detect when something abnormal occurs. Whenever in doubt, though, call your clinic.

Early signs of ill health

One of the first signs of ill health may be a subtle change in your dog's normal behaviour. It may be quieter than usual, less active, or disinclined to go for a walk. It may be thirstier, or less hungry. Since dogs, like humans, have their 'off' days, you should keep an eye on this sort of change for a day or two. If it continues, then take further action.

Consult your veterinarian if your dog shows any of the following signs:
- Unusual tiredness or lethargy
- Abnormal discharges from body openings
- Excessive head shaking
- Excessive scratching, licking or biting at any part of the body
- Markedly increased or decreased appetite
- Excessive water consumption
- Difficult, abnormal or uncontrolled waste elimination
- Marked weight loss or weight gain
- Abnormal behaviour such as hyperactivity, aggression or lethargy
- Abnormal swellings on any part of the body
- Lameness
- Difficulty in getting up or down.

As soon as you see anything unusual, make a note of it, for you may need this information if you take your dog to a veterinarian at a later date. While doctors talk to their human patients for a 'history', vets cannot do the same with their patients; they rely on the pet owner.

Pain

Pain results from the stimulation of specialised nerve endings (receptors) in the body. It has many causes, but is usually the result of injury, infection, poisoning, or inflammatory reaction. It is one of the earliest signs of disease.

If we suffer pain, we are able to tell someone. A dog cannot speak, but there are ways in which it can demonstrate how it feels. Some dogs, particularly those of the smaller breeds, react to the slightest incident; others, especially the hounds, are rather more stoical, but in most cases your dog's reactions will be fairly clear.

It will usually yelp in pain if you accidentally step on its foot or something has struck it. It may cry out if you touch a very painful part of its body, and even snap at you. However,

TOP: A vet is able to detect ill health by looking at the eyes of this 12-week-old Border Collie.

sometimes the only indication that something is wrong may be a less obvious change in its behaviour.

○ If it has hurt a leg it may put the foot of the affected leg on the ground but place no weight on it, limp, or carry the leg off the ground.

○ If it is suffering from joint pain, for example from arthritis, it may cry out when getting up or lying down.

○ Cramp will cause muscle tremors, and the dog may whimper.

○ Pain or irritation from its anal glands will cause it to 'scoot' its bottom along the ground. The dog may turn and frequently inspect the painful hind-end.

○ Pain in an eye will cause it to paw at the affected area or rub it against objects.

○ Pain in an ear usually results in the dog tilting its head to the affected side, and shaking it frequently.

○ Mouth pain may cause salivation, and the dog may yawn frequently.

○ It can be more difficult to detect when a dog is suffering spinal, head or internal pain.

Suspect spinal pain if your dog:

○ seems to be lame, but no limb is affected

○ resents being touched along its back

○ humps its back and/or trembles when standing up

○ is incontinent

○ has difficulty assuming normal posture for defecation

○ collapses on its hind quarters.

Suspect head pain if your dog:

○ has half-closed eyes, but no obvious eye problem

○ presses the top of its head against objects

○ gently but regularly shakes its head

○ stares vacantly.

Suspect internal pain if your dog:

○ spends more time lying down, and/or lies in a curled up position

○ is particularly restless, and unable to settle down

○ keeps its abdominal muscles tensed or stands in a hunched-up position

○ adopts a 'prayer' position, with forelegs down and hind legs up

○ continually looks around at its abdomen, or bites or licks at it

○ continually strains to pass a bowel movement, but fails

○ is usually docile and inexplicably becomes aggressive.

What to do: If the pain was caused by a minor accident (for example if someone stepped on the dog's toe), use common sense and monitor the outcome. If pain persists after a few hours, contact your vet. If pain is the result of something more serious, or you can't determine the cause, seek veterinary advice.

Cleaning your dog's ears

All dogs have some hair at the entrance to their ears, so regularly pluck out any excess hairs with your fingers (don't go too deep). Use round-ended scissors to trim away excess hair inside the ear flap.

Dogs sometimes scratch at one or both ears because they contain accumulated wax. This excess of wax can be due to hair blocking the ear canal, or a response to a minor irritation. If the ears are not inflamed or painful you can clean them yourself.

Use an ear-cleaning solution recommended by your vet. Twice daily, gently flood the ear canal with the fluid, massage externally, then wipe away excessive fluid and wax using cotton wool balls. Do not use any form of powder, or push anything down into the ear canal.

If the dog is still shaking its head after four to five days of this treatment, or if there is any inflammation or pain, see your vet.

ABOVE: A vet checks for joint and spinal pain in this young mixed-breed dog.
TOP: Use a round-ended pair of scissors to trim excess hair, so as not to hurt the dog.

Ear problems

SIGNS	POSSIBLE CAUSES	ACTION
Shaking head, black material in ear canal	Excessive wax accumulation	Clean ear(s) as on p97
Shaking head, scratching ears, gritty blackish discharge	Ear mites	Take to the vet to confirm (see p93, Ear mites)
Shaking head, reddish or yellowish-white, smelly discharge. Ear canal and inside of ear flap may be inflamed. Ear painful to touch	External ear infection (*otitis externa*). This is usually caused by a mixture of bacteria, fungi and yeasts. If left untreated it can cause severe pain and discomfort and lead to permanent ear damage	Do not place anything into the ear because the ear drum may be ruptured and some treatments may be harmful if they enter the middle ear. Take the dog to the vet, who will check that the ear drum (tympanic membrane) is intact, and may take a swab for culture to determine which infective organisms are present. Follow prescribed treatment
Shaking head, rubbing head on carpet, no obvious discharge, dog distressed, head held on one side	Foreign body in the ear canal, commonly a grass seed	Take the dog to the vet, who will remove the foreign body. Do not feed the dog prior to the appointment, as it may need a sedative
Head tilted to one side, loss of balance, abnormal movement of eyeballs (nystagmus). Dog may be vomiting	Middle- and inner-ear disease (*otitis media* and *otitis interna*). Can result from a foreign body or chronic ear infection	Take to the vet. Once the cause has been established, treatment may involve anti-inflammatory drugs, antibiotics and drugs (anti-emetics) to stop any vomiting
	Old dog vestibular syndrome. The cause is uncertain; it occurs suddenly in older dogs and responds to anti-inflammatory drugs.	Take to the vet
Swelling of the ear flap. Affected ear may be tilted downwards, and the head shaken	Aural haematoma. This is a build-up of blood or fluid between the cartilage and the skin of the ear flap. The cause is uncertain, but may be due to the dog shaking its head or scratching at the ear flap. It may also be the result of an auto-immune reaction	Wait 48 hours to allow time for the fluid to have finished accumulating, then take the dog to your vet. The vet may treat the condition medically or surgically. Treatment will involve draining the fluid and replacing it with antibiotics and anti-inflammatory drugs. With surgical treatment, under general anaesthetic, the area is opened and drained, then stitched to prevent fluid build-up
Superficial scabs on white ears; reddened skin	Sunburn	Purchase paediatric sunblock from your pharmacist and apply it to the affected areas three times daily Try to keep the dog in the shade during the hours of most intense sunlight
Deep, long-standing scabs that have never healed	Cancer of the ear (squamous cell carcinoma)	Take to the vet. Treatment may involve cryosurgery (freezing with liquid nitrogen) or surgical removal of the pinna (ear flap)

Ear problems *(continued)*

SIGNS	POSSIBLE CAUSES	ACTION
Dog appears deaf	Wax blocking ear canal Inner ear infection (*otitis media, otitis interna*) Congenital defect Old age	Get a veterinary check to establish precise cause

Mouth and oesophagus problems

SIGNS	POSSIBLE CAUSES	ACTION
Bad breath	Tartar build up on teeth	Take to the vet. It will probably need to have its teeth scaled and polished
Bad breath, inflamed, bleeding gums	Gingivitis (inflammation of gums)	As above. Antibiotics may be necessary
Difficulty in eating, bad breath	Broken or infected tooth	Take to the vet. The tooth will need extraction; antibiotics may be needed
As above, may be bleeding, drooling tongue may be displaced	Tumour in the mouth (eg melanoma)	Take to the vet for assessment
Visible swelling under tongue	Ranula (blocked salivary duct)	Take to the vet
Drooling, pawing at mouth, may be gulping	Foreign body (eg bone or stick) lodged across the hard palate between upper molar teeth, or fish hook in lip	Open the mouth and check. If a foreign body is present and you can remove it, do so. Take care not to get bitten. If damage has occurred, or you can't find the cause of the problem, take the dog to the vet
	Bee sting in mouth (on tongue, inside cheeks or gum)	If you can see the sting, try to remove it with tweezers. Check the mouth regularly, and if more than slight swelling occurs, take the dog to the vet
	Ulcerated tongue	Check the tongue. If inflamed or ulcerated, investigate access to irritant or corrosive poisons. Take a sample of the suspected substance to the vet. See pp48–9, Poisons
Drooling, retching or coughing	Object stuck in the throat Kennel cough	Take to the vet in both instances
Regurgitating food, may be retching and salivating	Object stuck in the oesophagus Inflamed oesophagus	Take to the vet in both instances
Difficulty in eating, no other signs	Nerve problem	Take to the vet for diagnosis

Stomach problems

SIGNS	SOME POSSIBLE CAUSES	ACTION
Eating grass, then vomiting grass and mucus (and bone)	Natural evacuation of indigestible material	Carry out protocol for vomiting in both instances (see p49, Emergency treatment)
As above, no bone	Mild gastritis	
Vomiting frequently, refusing food, depressed	Gastritis Pancreatitis	Take to the vet Take to the vet, URGENTLY
As above, plus other possible signs including diarrhoea (with or without blood), dark tarry faeces	Bacterial infection from rotting or infected food Canine parvovirus infection Gastric ulceration Poisoning	Take to the vet in all instances
As above, plus hunched posture	Foreign body lodged in stomach Pancreatitis	Take to the vet Take to the vet, URGENTLY
Distended abdomen, young dog, may be lethargic, poor coat	Worm burden	Treat for worms (see pp85-90)
Distended abdomen, retching, laboured breathing	Gastric dilation or torsion. The stomach has become filled with gas after eating or over-eating, and may then have twisted round, blocking off the routes of entry and exit. More commonly seen in deep-chested breeds, eg Boxer, German Shepherd and Weimaraner, especially if the dog is exercised too soon after eating	URGENT ACTION REQUIRED Get veterinary help immediately. Surgery may be needed

Assessing and treating vomiting

In dogs, vomiting is a natural way of eliminating material from the stomach, and does not necessarily indicate a problem.

If your dog vomits once or twice but otherwise appears bright, offer water only and monitor for four hours. If no more vomiting occurs, offer a small amount of bland food (such as cooked chicken and rice). If all is well, feed the bland food over the next 24 hours, then gradually reintroduce its normal diet.

Consult your vet if you are in any doubt, or if:

- the dog appears depressed
- there is blood in the vomit
- the dog is vomiting intermittently (eg every three to four hours) for more than eight hours
- the dog is vomiting continuously and cannot keep water down
- the dog has had access to household rubbish or poisonous substances.

Intestinal problems

SIGNS	SOME POSSIBLE CAUSES	ACTION
Eating well but remaining thin	Worm burden	Treat for worms (see pp85-90)
As above, passing large amounts of pale faeces, may be eating own faeces	Exocrine pancreatic insufficiency	Take to the vet
Salivating or drooling, no other symptoms Salivation with weight loss, faeces appear normal or could have diarrhoea, vomiting	Inflammatory bowel disease. Several causes, which result in inflammation of the bowel and a reduction in its ability to absorb nutrients. May also be an associated bacterial overgrowth (abnormally high proliferation of certain bacteria).	Take to the vet
Eating excessively, may be eating unusual things	Exocrine pancreatic insufficiency. Malabsorption syndrome (inability to absorb nutrients properly) Anaemia	Take to the vet in all instances
Flatulence	Usually dietary, but also associated with old age. More common in certain breeds	Feed a highly digestible, low-fibre, moderately low protein, soy-free, wheat-free diet
Chronic weight loss despite normal or increased appetite	Worms Tumour in bowel Malabsorption syndrome	Take to the vet to confirm cause
As above, intermittent vomiting and/or diarrhoea	Inflammatory bowel disease (see above)	Take to the vet
As above, but large amounts of grey or putty-coloured faeces	Exocrine pancreatic insufficiency	Take to the vet
Vomiting, not eating	Inflammatory bowel disease (see above) Foreign body Severe constipation	Take to the vet in all instances
Hunched-up posture	Abdominal pain Severe constipation	Take to the vet in both instances
Straining to defecate, hard firm faeces, straining ceases after passage of faeces, not vomiting	Mild constipation, particularly common in elderly dogs	Give mineral oil (1 teaspoon to 1 tablespoon, depending on dog size). If faeces are not passed within eight hours, take to the vet.
Constantly straining to defecate, few or no faeces produced, depressed, possibly vomiting	Severe constipation Prostate swelling preventing passage of faeces	Take to the vet to ascertain cause

Intestinal problems *(continued)*

SIGNS	SOME POSSIBLE CAUSES	ACTION
Continuous straining, swelling at side of anus	Perineal hernia	Take to the vet. Surgical treatment is needed
Pain during defecation, 'scooting' bottom along floor, looking at and/or licking rear end. May be a discharge of pus	Anal gland impaction, inflammation or abscess	Take to the vet for treatment, which may include flushing out the affected gland(s) and treatment with antibiotics
Fresh blood in faeces	Colitis (inflammation of colon) Tumour Anal gland abscess	Take to the vet in all instances
Diarrhoea, one or two bouts, without blood, dog otherwise bright and alert, no vomiting	Food intolerance Mild bacterial enteritis	Offer water only for one day, then bland diet for 24 hours. If diarrhoea stops, gradually re-introduce normal diet. If diarrhoea continues, see the vet
Diarrhoea, intermittent, may be round-worms in faeces	Roundworm infestation	Treat for roundworms (see pp85-86)
Diarrhoea, frequent and persistent, dog otherwise bright	Giardiasis (*Giardia* infection) Coccidiosis	Take to the vet in both instances
Diarrhoea, frequent, may be blood, dog depressed and may have abdominal pain	Enteritis: bacterial (eg *Leptospira haemorrhagiae*) or viral (eg Canine Parvovirus, Canine Distemper, Infectious Canine Hepatitis. See pp81-83) Inflammatory bowel disease (see above) Malabsorption syndrome (inability to absorb nutrients) Colitis Tumour	Take to the vet in all instances

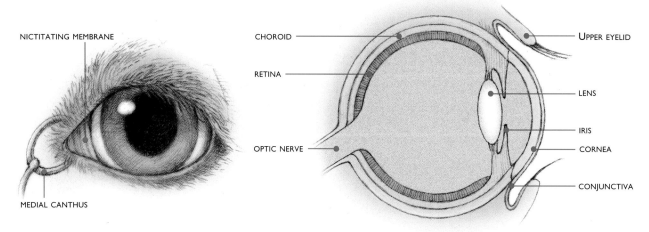

Although similar to the human eye, the dog has a higher number of light-sensitive cells as well as a nictitating membrane, like a cat

Endocrine problems

SIGNS	SOME POSSIBLE CAUSES	ACTION
Abdominal enlargement, excessive thirst, symmetrical hair loss, pigment changes	Hyperadrenocorticism or Cushing's syndrome (excessive hormone production from adrenal gland)	Take to the vet
Lethargy, off food, may be vomiting, weight loss, middle-aged female	Hypoadrenocorticism or Addison's disease (inadequate hormone production from adrenal gland)	Take to the vet
Young dog, poor growth	Hypothyroidism (lack of thyroid hormone)	Take to the vet
Older dog, lethargy, obesity, intolerant of cold, poor hair growth		
Neck swelling, hyperactive, increased appetite, excessive thirst, increased urine output, panting	Hyperthyroidism (excess of thyroid hormone)	Take to the vet

Eye problems

SIGNS	SOME POSSIBLE CAUSES	ACTION
Avoiding light, blinking	Several	Take to the vet
Runny eyes, clear discharge	Wind, dust, strong sunlight, allergy or blocked tear duct. Some dogs may be born without a tear duct	Bathe with cooled, boiled water or ophthalmic saline. If it doesn't clear in a few days, take to the vet
As above, sudden onset, eyelids swollen, may be rubbing at face Runny eyes, clear discharge, inflamed conjunctiva	Urticaria (acute allergy to sting or other allergen) Hair rubbing on eye (trichiasis or districhiasis) Entropion (in-turned eyelid)	Take to the vet in all instances
As above, dog coughing Runny eyes, clear or purulent discharge, bottom lid appears to be gaping, conjunctiva very inflamed Runny eyes, purulent discharge, whites of eyes inflamed, pawing at eyes As above, hair loss around eyes As above, one eye only	Kennel cough Ectropion (out-turned eyelid) Bacterial or viral conjunctivitis Canine Distemper Infectious Canine Hepatitis *Demodex* infection Possible foreign body in eye, or injury to eye	Take to the vet in all instances
Tacky, purulent discharge. Eyes seem dry. Conjunctiva inflamed	Dry eye (keratoconjunctivitis sicca)	Take to the vet
Growth of tissue over cornea, may appear brownish	Pannus	Take to the vet
Eyes appear white, dog's vision appears to be affected	Cataract formation	Take to the vet

Eye problems *(continued)*

SIGNS	SOME POSSIBLE CAUSES	ACTION
Dog appears to be going blind, no other symptoms	Retinal degeneration Progressive Retinal Atrophy (inherited) Collie Eye Anomaly (congenital)	Take to the vet in all instances
Reddish lump in corner of eye, young dog. Common in Bulldogs	'Cherry eye'. Excessive tissue growth on third eyelid	This will need surgery. Take to the vet
Area of skin with hair growing out of it, on conjunctiva and/or cornea and lids	Ocular dermoid (growth)	Take to the vet. This requires surgery
Small growth on upper or lower eyelid	Periocular granuloma	May need surgery. Take to the vet
Dog closing one eye, may be avoiding light, apparent pain, eye watering	Inflammation within the eye (uveitis)	Take to the vet
As above, white line or dot on the surface of the eye, pain, eye watering	Corneal ulcer. Often the result of a cat scratch	Take to the vet
Third eyelid showing	Nerve damage	Take to the vet
Pressing head against objects (sign of headache), eye appears protruding, avoids light	Glaucoma (swelling of the eyeball due to accumulation of fluid causing increased pressure)	Take to the vet

Liver, spleen or pancreatic problems

SIGNS	SOME POSSIBLE CAUSES	ACTION
Abdominal distension, with or without jaundice	Liver tumour	Take to the vet
Abdominal distension, excessive thirst, pale gums, lethargy	Tumour of spleen causing internal bleeding	Take to the vet
Vomiting, jaundiced, dark urine, may be abdominal pain, poor appetite	Bile duct blockage (bile stones, bile sludging, inflammation, infection) Bile duct rupture	Take to the vet in both instances
Vomiting, diarrhoea, jaundice, blood in urine	Leptospirosis (see p83)	Take to the vet
Off-colour, lethargic, fever, bloody diarrhoea	Infectious Canine Hepatitis (see p82)	Take to the vet
Acute, persistent vomiting, fever, abdominal pain	Pancreatitis. Pancreatic digestive enzymes may be secreted into the pancreatic tissue itself, causing severe inflammation and tissue destruction. Can cause widespread damage and death. Recovered animals may suffer permanent dysfunction of the gland	Take to the vet

Liver, spleen or pancreatic problems *(continued)*

SIGNS	SOME POSSIBLE CAUSES	ACTION
Dry scaly coat; weight loss; large quantities of light-coloured, soft, smelly faeces; coprophagia (eating own faeces)	Exocrine Pancreatic Insufficiency (EPI). Some or all of the part of the pancreas that secretes digestive enzymes is missing. Digestion of fats, particularly, is difficult, and faeces contain large amounts of water and undigested fat. Fatty acid deficiency causes a dry, scaly coat. EPI is usually congenital, but may become apparent later in life (prevalent in German Shepherd Dogs)	Consult your vet, who will test a faeces sample from the dog. The usual treatment is enzymes, mainly trypsin, in tablet or powder form, and adjust the diet to include extra vitamin supplements and highly digestible oils (safflower or coconut)
Excessive thirst, hunger, may be abdominal enlargement, lethargy, weight loss	Diabetes mellitus. If the pancreas does not produce enough insulin, the result is diabetes mellitus. Glucose levels build up in the bloodstream (especially after meals). This results in glucose passing through the kidneys and into the urine, taking water with it. Breeds prone to diabetes include the Dachshund, King Charles Spaniel, Poodle (all types) and Scottish Terrier	Take your dog for a thorough check-up, including blood and urine tests. Mild cases may be controlled by adjusting the diet. In most cases diabetes mellitus can be controlled only by regular injections of insulin. These can be given at home

Hypoglycaemic coma may occur in a dog receiving insulin injections if it is subject to excessive activity or exercise or goes for a long time between feeds. Inadequate glucose levels in the bloodstream are further lowered by the action of the injected insulin, leading to collapse, coma and convulsions. Treatment: give glucose or honey by mouth (always keep these substances on hand in case of an emergency) |

Nervous system problems

SIGNS	SOME POSSIBLE CAUSES	ACTION
Loss of balance, lack of coordination	Middle-ear infection
Vestibular disease (infection, inflammation or tumour affecting the vestibule)
Brain tumour
Disease of cerebellum	Take to the vet in all instances
Seizures or convulsions	Epilepsy (more common in dogs up to three years old)
Poisoning (see pp48–9)
Brain tumour	Take to the vet in all instances

Nervous system problems *(continued)*

SIGNS	SOME POSSIBLE CAUSES	ACTION
Fits, convulsions, head pressing, head pain	Inflammatory reaction of brain (encephalitis) Inflammatory reaction of brain lining (meningitis)	URGENT ACTION NEEDED Take to the vet
Collapsing, third eyelids visible, limbs rigid, tail straight, face contracting	Tetanus infection	Take to the vet
Salivating, may be other signs Salivating, behaviour change	Poisoning (see pp48–9) Rabies (see pp83-4)	Take to the vet
Abnormal head position (eg tilt), eyes may be flicking from side to side	Middle ear disease Vestibular disease (infection, inflammation or tumour affecting the vestibule) Brain tumour	Take to the vet
As above, old dog	Old dog vestibular syndrome (disease affecting the vestibule)	Take to the vet
Wobbling gait, scuffing feet, unsteady on feet especially after exercise (common in Bassets, Doberman, Great Dane)	Wobbler syndrome (cervical spondylopathy). Due to malformation of one or more cervical vertebrae causing bruising to spinal cord in neck	Treatment may be successful if caught early, otherwise prognosis very poor
Reluctant to move head, acute pain in neck	Cervical disc protrusion	Take to the vet
Collapsing in hindquarters, with or without acute pain	Disc protrusion in thoracic or lumbar region	Take to the vet
Weakness or collapse after exercise	Myasthenia gravis (neuromuscular disorder)	Take to the vet
Sudden collapse, walking in circles, partial paralysis, eyelids partly closed, eyes flickering	Stroke	Take to the vet

What to do if your dog is lame

You may be able to deal with some causes of lameness, but most will require veterinary attention. If you wish, you can use the following protocol to help you detect what area of a limb may be affected and get an idea of what the problem may be.

If the cause is not obvious, you can gently check the affected limb for signs of injury. First inspect the pads for an injury such as a cut or an embedded thorn. If nothing is visible, gently press each pad in turn to detect any painful area. Then, beginning at the toes, gradually work up the leg. As you do so, apply gentle pressure with your fingers and check your dog's response. When you reach an injured area your dog will probably react because the pressure is causing pain. To detect joint pain, gently manipulate each joint in turn.

If you are in any doubt as to what the cause is, or what to do, contact your vet.

Skeletal, joint and muscle problems

SIGNS	SOME POSSIBLE CAUSES	ACTION
Slight lameness on one limb, one joint mildly painful when flexed or extended	Sprain (slight damage to ligament or cartilage in a joint)	Apply a cold compress, then use a crepe bandage to support limb. A severe sprain can lead to arthritis, so if doesn't improve within 24 hours or if you are in doubt, get veterinary advice
Lameness hours after exercise, can bear weight on the foot of the affected leg	Muscle strain	Rest for two days. Gentle massage may help. If no improvement, take to the vet
Sudden lameness, cries if foot touched, toenail may be bleeding	Torn toenail	Take to the vet for trimming and antibiotics
Sudden lameness, reluctant to walk on hard surface, recent prolonged exercise on roads	Skinned pads	Exercise only on soft surfaces. Apply lanolin to affected areas. Use a spray to harden the pad
Sudden lameness, bleeding foot	Cut pad	If superficial, bathe in saline solution or cetrimide solution (1:20 dilution). Keep off hard surfaces for two weeks. If deep, take to the vet for stitching
Sudden lameness or acute pain during or after vigorous exercise, muscle tremors, unwilling to move, may be crying	Myositis. Inflammation of the muscles with severe pain, swelling and difficulty in moving. Commonly occurs as cramp, caused by build-up of lactic acid in muscles after strenuous exercise and rapid cooling down (eg by jumping into cold water). Sometimes affects hind-leg muscles of Greyhounds during racing	Massage the affected limb and keep the dog warm. If pain persists, consult a vet
Similar to above, in Scottish or Cairn terrier. Dog takes short, jerky steps. May involve the muscles of the forelegs and neck, with the dog unable to move	Scotty Cramp	Let the dog rest. The condition usually subsides after a few minutes. Discuss with your vet
Muscles on each side of the jaw swollen, mouth held open, dog in pain, eats with difficulty	Eosinophilic myositis. German Shepherds are particularly susceptible. Affects jaw muscles involved in eating. Onset is usually abrupt. Attacks last one to three weeks, time between attacks varies from three weeks to six months. Attacks become less severe but more frequent; after each attack the affected muscles become more atrophied	Get veterinary advice. It is a painful and progressive disease for which no cure has been found, although painkillers and anti-inflammatory drugs can help reduce the severity of an attack

SIGNS	SOME POSSIBLE CAUSES	ACTION
Sudden lameness on one hind leg after vigorous exercise, touching toe to ground but not bearing weight on it	Ruptured anterior cruciate ligament in knee joint. A comparatively common injury that usually occurs as the result of an accident, such as slipping. Some dogs are more likely to sustain this injury because of the shape of their bones	Take to the vet, as surgery will probably be needed
Sudden lameness, holding one hind leg off the ground, yelping	Slipped knee cap (patella)	Take to the vet
Sudden lameness, hind limb twisted and painful	Hip dislocation	Take to the vet
Sudden lameness after fall or accident, swelling , pain, may be yelping	Bone fracture	Take to the vet
Sudden lameness, swelling of leg tissue	Bite wound	Take to the vet. The wound may be forming an abscess
'Bunny-hopping' gait, young animal	Hip dysplasia. Can be congenital or inherited. The head of the femur does not fit properly into the socket (acetabulum), so abnormal wear occurs in the joint, resulting in degeneration. German Shepherds and Labradors are more prone, and in many countries breeding dogs are screened for hip dysplasia in an attempt to eliminate the disease.	Take to the vet. This is a painful condition that cannot be cured other than by surgery
Sudden hind limb collapse, dog usually in pain	Intervertebral disc protrusion in thoracic or lumbar region	Request a house call. Or slide the dog onto a board and restrict movement, then take to the vet
Difficulty getting up or down, activity eases stiffness	Arthritis (degenerative joint disease)	Take to the vet
Difficulty in assuming normal posture for urination	Spondylosis (degenerative condition resulting in deposition of extra bone between vertebrae)	Take to the vet
Difficulty getting up and down, depressed, doesn't improve with exercise, off food	Spondylitis (infection of bone in one or more vertebrae)	Take to the vet
	Bone cancer, usually spread from prostate cancer	Take to the vet
Swelling of one or more joints, dog depressed, sometimes off food, lame and lethargic	Arthritis (infectious or immune-mediated)	Take to the vet

Some common skeletal, joint and muscle problems *(continued)*

SIGNS	SOME POSSIBLE CAUSES	ACTION
Firm, painful swelling just above a joint, becoming larger over time; large dog	Bone cancer Osteomyelitis (bone infection)	Take to the vet Take to the vet
Acute fore limb lameness, neck pain, reluctant to move head	Cervical (neck) disc protrusion	Take to the vet
Chronic lameness affecting front leg in large breeds (eg German Shepherd or Labrador Retriever)	Elbow dysplasia (inherited condition) Arthritis (degenerative joint disease)	Take to the vet

Some common skin problems

SIGNS	SOME POSSIBLE CAUSES	ACTION
Scaly skin, white flakes within the coat	*Cheyletiella* (mite) infection (see pp93-94)	Ask vet for an insecticidal treatment
Scurfy skin, particularly around head and shoulders, may be itchy. Tiny, greyish-white insects visible	Lice (see p93)	As above
Hair loss, symmetrical, no irritation, no broken hairs	Hormonal imbalance	Get veterinary advice
Bald areas, not symmetrical, no irritation, no broken hairs	Prolonged or excessive moult Dietary (fatty acid) deficiency	Take to the vet
Hair loss, not symmetrical, broken hairs visible, dog may react with a scratch reflex when its skin is rubbed	Self-inflicted through scratching, probably in response to an allergen	Take to the vet to determine the cause
Hair loss around eyes and possibly other parts of body. May be itchy. Pustules may be present	Demodectic mange)	Take to the vet
Hair loss over a raised, pinkish area of skin. Not itchy	Ringworm (fungal infection)	Take to the vet
Scratching, skin reddened, oily, smelly and scaly	Yeast infection	Take to the vet
Scratching, excessive licking	Allergy to fleas, food, or something in the environment	If you flea control is adequate,take to the vet. If it isn't, treat for fleas (see pp91-93)
Scratching, chewing feet, late summer	Harvest mites (*Trombicula autumnalis*)	Ask vet for an insecticidal treatment
Scratching, chewing, hair loss on elbow region and feet	Mange (*Sarcoptes scabei*)	Take to the vet
Scratching, excessive licking, skin rash on underside of abdomen and inner thighs	Contact allergy Flea allergy	Take to the vet

Skin problems *(continued)*

SIGNS	SOME POSSIBLE CAUSES	ACTION
Scratching, chewing, area inflamed and with pus, may be bleeding	Pyoderma (deep bacterial infection)	Take to the vet
Lump or swelling within the skin. Not painful	Lipoma (fatty tumour) Haematoma (blood blister) Skin tumour Sebaceous cyst	Take to the vet in each instance
Lump or swelling within the skin. Painful. May be discharging fluid	Abscess	Take to the vet
Persistent skin lesions around lips and feet, not itchy	Auto-immune condition	Take to the vet

Some signs of urinary problems

SIGNS	SOME POSSIBLE CAUSES	ACTION
Vomiting, abdominal pain, bad breath, straining, blood in urine	Acute kidney disease (nephritis)	URGENT ACTION REQUIRED. Get to the vet immediately
Excessive thirst, bad breath, dog may be passing large quantities of urine, may be mouth ulcers, weight loss, anaemia	Chronic kidney disease (nephritis) resulting from an infection, chronic degeneration, tumour or inherited defect	Measure and note the dog's water intake over a course of a day. Collect a sample of urine in a clean container, and take this with you to the vet for analysis.
Young dog, failing to thrive, excessive thirst, very pale urine	Juvenile renal disease (inherited)	Collect a sample of urine. Take sample and dog to the vet
Strong-smelling urine, with or without blood, frequent urination or leaking, may lick vulva or penis	Cystitis (inflammation of bladder) due to infection or bladder stones	Collect a sample of urine as above. Take sample and dog to the vet
Urine leaking from vulva or penis (urinary incontinence) As above, male dog As above, old dog	Sphincter incompetence due to hormonal or nerve problem Prostate problem Old age	Take to the vet in each instance
Male dog, straining to pass urine, may be vomiting	Urethral blockage, possibly by a bladder stone	URGENT ACTION REQUIRED. Take to the vet immediately

Some signs of blood and circulatory system problems

SIGNS	SOME POSSIBLE CAUSES	ACTION
Exercise intolerance and/or lethargy, weakness, possibly fainting. Puppy or young dog	Congenital malformation allows shunting of blood within the heart but by-passing the lungs (patent ductus arteriosus)	Take to the vet in each instance
As above, any age	Heart valve defect. Blood flows back through a valve, causing a heart murmur	
As above, any age	Anaemia	
Coughing	Congestive heart failure (chronic heart disease)	Take to the vet in each instance
	Heart-based tumour	
	Heartworm disease (see pp89-90)	
Abnormal breathing	Anaemia	Take to the vet in each instance
	Lung congestion due to malfunctioning heart	
	Warfarin poisoning	
Pale or bluish tinge to gums	Malfunctioning heart	Take to the vet in each instance
	Haemolytic anaemia (abnormal destruction of red blood cells)	
	Warfarin poisoning	
	Blood clotting disorder	
Jaundice (yellow tinge to gums and whites of eyes)	Haemolytic anaemia (abnormal destruction of red blood cells)	Take to the vet in each instance
	Secondary liver infection	
Abdominal distension	Fluid accumulation due to malfunctioning heart	Take to the vet

Laboured breathing

If breathing is laboured, and/or there is abdominal movement associated with it, take the dog to a vet immediately.

THIS IS AN EMERGENCY

Respiratory system problems

SIGNS	SOME POSSIBLE CAUSES	ACTION
Sneezing, clear nasal discharge	Viral infection, allergy (eg to pollen), grass seed or blade of grass lodged in nose or a tumour	If persistent, take the dog to the vet
Sneezing, purulent nasal discharge from one or both nostrils	Bacterial or fungal infection	Take to the vet
	Molar abscess	
Dry crusty nose	Zinc deficiency	Take to the vet
	Allergy (eg to pollen)	
Red, puffy skin on nose, with some crusting	Sunburn	If nose is red and sore, keep out of the sun. Apply paediatric sunblock. If problem does not subside, take to the vet
	Allergy (eg to pollen)	

SIGNS	SOME POSSIBLE CAUSES	ACTION
Noisy breathing, short-nosed breed (especially Cavalier King Charles Spaniel)	Elongated soft palate. A congenital defect. The floppy palate partly obstructs the larynx, interferes with respiration, and causes snorting while breathing.	Take to the vet for assessment
Noisy breathing, any breed. May be change in tone of the bark	Laryngeal problem (eg laryngitis)	Take to the vet
Choking, collapse, short-nosed breed	Elongated soft palate causing complete obstruction to breathing	URGENT ACTION REQUIRED. Open the mouth, extend head and neck, pull out tongue and gently press the chest to get the dog breathing
Choking, collapse, any breed	Foreign body in throat obstructing breathing	Try to remove the obstruction. Get urgent veterinary help
Rapid breathing	Pneumonia Heart problem Allergic asthma Poisoning (eg aspirin) Worm larvae migrating through the lungs	Take to the vet
As above, gums pale or white	Internal or external haemorrhage Poisoning (eg warfarin)	URGENT ACTION. Take to the vet
Abdominal movement associated with breathing	Diaphragmatic hernia (rupture of diaphragm after trauma) Pneumothorax (air in the chest, usually after trauma) Haemothorax (blood in chest) after anticoagulant (rat poison) poisoning Rib/lung damage after trauma	Take to the vet in each instance
Bleeding from nose	Acute trauma Foreign body in nose Problem with clotting mechanism Poisoning with rodenticide (eg warfarin) Tumour	Initially, place an ice pack (a packet of frozen vegetables) on the top of the nose. If bleeding continues, take to the vet Take to the vet in each instance
Mild, occasional coughing	Tracheitis, allergy or a heart problem	Take to the vet
Frequent shallow coughing, has had a recent accident	Pneumothorax (air in chest)	Take to the vet
Coughing, frequent, honking	Tracheal collapse	Take to the vet. Usually treated by surgery
Frequent coughing, progressing to retching, white foam produced	Kennel cough or a foreign body in throat	Take to the vet
Frequent coughing, harsh, associated purulent nasal discharge, dog appears ill	Canine distemper	Take to the vet

Stages and duration of oestrus cycle

PRO-OESTRUS	OESTRUS	MET-OESTRUS	ANOESTRUS
Vulva swollen with blood-stained discharge Bitch attractive to dogs but will not allow mating	Vulva very enlarged, discharge more straw-coloured. Bitch will allow mating. Ovulation occurs about two days after onset of oestrus.	Occurs in unmated bitch. No external signs. Hormone changes equivalent to pregnancy. Around six to eight weeks after the end of oestrus a bitch may show signs of pyometra (see below) Around eight to nine weeks after the end of oestrus a bitch may show signs of false pregnancy	Sexual inactivity
Variable length Average nine days	Variable length Average nine days	Variable length Average 90 days	Variable length Average 90 days

Some signs of reproductive problems in the bitch

SIGNS	SOME POSSIBLE CAUSES	ACTION
Milky discharge from vulva, young puppy	Puppy vaginitis (mild inflammation of the vagina)	Usually self-curative. If in doubt, talk to your vet
Persistent thin, light-red discharge from vulva after oestrous cycle	Ovarian cyst	Take to the vet
Excessive thirst, reduced appetite, vomiting, distended abdomen, vulval discharge, six to eight weeks after oestrous cycle	Pyometra (fluid accumulation in uterus). Cause may be a hormonal imbalance	URGENT ACTION. Take to vet. May need surgical removal of uterus and ovaries
Enlarged mammary gland, not painful Enlarged mammary gland, painful, inflamed	Mammary tumour. Not always malignant Mastitis	Take to the vet in each instance
Milk production without pregnancy, bitch may be 'nesting' and protecting toys, may pant and/or appear nervous	False pregnancy (pseudopregnancy). Occurs in about 60% of non-neutered bitches. After one false pregnancy, she is likely to have one after each oestrous cycle	Distract bitch with increased exercise and play. Remove toys. If persists after about three weeks, contact vet. May need hormone treatment
Lethargy, loss of appetite, within a week or two of whelping. May be purulent discharge from the vulva	Metritis (inflammation of uterus)	Take to the vet. May need antibiotics, or bitch may need to be spayed

Reproductive problems in the male

SIGNS	SOME POSSIBLE CAUSES	ACTION
Purulent discharge from penile sheath	Balanoposthitis (bacterial infection of sheath)	Clean the area daily with cooled boiled water and cotton wool. If discharge persists after five days, may need antibiotics
Enlarged testicle. May have symmetrical hair loss	Testicular tumour	Take to the vet for assessment
Spurting urination, blood in urine, straining to defecate	Prostate problem (tumour, abscess, enlargement), common in old dogs	Take to the vet for assessment

GROWING OLD
A happy retirement

Like humans, dogs are living longer as the result of better nutrition and health care. Expected life spans vary between breeds, but compared to 20 years ago the life expectancy of pet dogs has increased.

There are now more elderly dogs in the canine population needing special care. And with increasing old age comes a gradual deterioration in health. While nothing can be done to stop the body's aging processes, it is still possible to minimise their effects.

Signs of old age

Grey hairs and coat changes: One of the first signs of old age may be greying around the muzzle and eyebrows; however, this can occur in dogs as young as five years old, so it is not particularly significant.

In old age the coat tends to grow longer, even in short-coated breeds. The nails grow more quickly, too, so nail trimming is required more frequently.

Deep sleep: Another sign is increasingly deeper and more prolonged sleep. Old dogs are more likely to be startled if woken suddenly, and some may even growl or snap if suddenly woken by being touched.

○ Give your elderly dog a bed in a quiet, peaceful corner where it can relax in comfort.

○ Other pets should be kept away as much as possible.

Changes in feeding and drinking patterns:

○ Loss of appetite, reluctance to eat or difficulty in eating. The latter may be an indication of gum inflammation (gingivitis) and/or tooth decay.

○ Increasing thirst. This may be a sign of developing kidney disease or another health problem (see p110).

Old dogs may benefit from an adjustment to their diet, so that the food is more easily digested and contains lower protein levels to lessen any stress on their weakening kidneys. Special therapeutic diets are available from your veterinarian, who may advise more frequent health checks and routine blood samples to monitor kidney and liver function (see pp104 and 110.)

Digestive problems: Symptoms include vomiting, diarrhoea and constipation. Important changes to the diet may include:

○ three to four small meals daily (as for puppies)

○ cooked eggs (the most easily digested protein)

○ a prescription diet recommended by your veterinarian.

Arthritic changes and osteo-arthritis: Old dogs, and those that have been left to sleep on hard surfaces or out in cold conditions for long periods, are more likely to show this condition. An early sign is stiffness when

TOP: As dogs age, their muzzles may grey and they may suffer from osteo-arthritis, in the form of stiffness in the knee – just like their human companions.

getting up and first moving around, which then improves. In more extreme cases the dog has difficulty in walking, weakness on the hind legs, lameness and symptoms of pain (see pp96–97, Pain). As soon as you notice any signs, talk to your veterinarian and follow his or her advice.

Treatments include:

○ a daily non-steroidal, anti-inflammatory drug

○ drugs that aid the production of joint fluid

○ homeopathic and natural remedies, including substances such as glucosamine, as well as herbal remedies and shark cartilage.

Reduced bladder capacity and bladder control: One of the earliest signs of this may be that the dog needs to go out several times during the night. The dog also begins to lose control over its bladder (urinary incontinence), leaving puddles of urine on its bed or on the floor where it sits or lies down.

To keep it clean and comfortable, make up special bedding: place a plastic sheet on top of the bed, cover this with a thick wad of newspaper, and top with a polyester fur or sheepskin rug. Urine drains down through the rug and into the newspaper, leaving the top of the bed dry. The newspaper is easily changed as necessary.

ABOVE: If you are tolerant and sympathetic towards your elderly dog's changing needs, it will enjoy a happy and comfortable old age.

Constipation: Arthritic changes may prevent an old dog from adopting a normal excretory posture. Consider the following corrective measures:

o Increase the fibre in the diet by including bran or bran biscuits, and/or grated vegetables, and add a table spoonful of mineral oil as a lubricant.

o Change to a diet prescribed by your veterinarian.

Increasing deafness: In the early stages, deafness may be difficult to detect, as many dogs adapt quite well. Watch out for the following signs:

o Increased barking, usually for no apparent reason. This may occur while the dog is lying down on its bed.

o Barking in an altered voice, usually of a higher pitch.

o Failure to respond to your calls.

As your dog's hearing deteriorates, take special care to protect it from accidents. Keep it close to you during walks, and replace verbal calls with physical action – for example, instead of calling it back, go and fetch it.

Increasing blindness: During its early stages, deteriorating sight may not be detected. Later signs include:

o The eyeballs appear a bluish colour (cornea affected).

o The eye appears white in the centre (cataract).

o The dog may blunder into objects such as furniture.

o The dog is reluctant to go out at night and/or in bright sunlight.

Try not to move the furniture, and protect the dog from danger. A partially or completely blind dog can usually live a contented life as long it is in familiar surroundings.

Senility: Signs are:

o Disorientation

o Restlessness

o Increased demand for your attention

o Increased vocalisation.

Medication is now available to treat senility, so it is best to talk to your veterinarian.

Caring for an elderly dog

Just like old people, old dogs have good days and bad days. You will have to adapt, and be tolerant and sympathetic to the dog's needs. As the situation progresses you will probably need an increasing amount of involvement from your veterinarian, and medication may be required.

To reduce stress on your aging dog, supply a comfortable bed such as a polystyrene bean bag or sheepskin rug. Supply extra warmth through a heated pad, and don't allow your elderly dog to lie on rough surfaces. Because an old dog spends a lot of time lying down it develops calluses on its elbows and hocks. Rough surfaces can cause these to become inflamed and painful, and they may ulcerate.

You could also:

o Put comfortable blankets or rugs in its favourite lying places, out of full sun and away from damp areas.

o Avoid putting your dog out in very hot sun, or into very cold winter conditions.

o Dress it in a dog coat, even indoors.

o Protect it from situations in which it is likely to fall: for example, put barriers across steps or stairs, and make sure that it cannot fall from a sundeck.

o Hand massage its limbs to improve its mobility.

o Allow it to take the exercise it wants, rather than what you think it needs. Because its senses of sight and scent are deteriorating, it can become disoriented, so stay close to it when it is off the leash.

ABOVE: Musculo-skeletal problems are common in old age, and some dogs benefit from chiropractic treatment.

If your elderly dog shows less interest in eating, slightly warm the food or change the diet to something more palatable. Adjust its food intake according to its level of activity. As a dog takes less exercise, it tends to put on weight, and an overweight dog is more prone to heart disease and other health problems. Ask your veterinarian about diets that are formulated specially for various health conditions (see p40, Nutrition).

Monitor how much water your old dog is drinking. If the quantity appears to be increasing, talk to your vet. Take your dog for regular health checks. Booster vaccinations need to be kept up to date, teeth and gums checked and anal sacs emptied. Routine blood sampling may assist with health care.

Thinking about a replacement

As your dog begins to age, you may decide to bring a new, younger dog into the household. You will have to spend a little time on integrating the two animals, but it creates a transitional stage that may help you to cope with the impending loss of an old friend (see p66, Common behaviour problems).

You may, on the other hand, decide to wait. Nursing an old dog may be enough for you to cope with, without having to spend time with a younger one that needs a lot of attention and basic training.

If you are in any doubt, talk to your veterinarian or the staff at your veterinary clinic.

The final days

This can be the most difficult period of your relationship with your dog, yet in many ways is one of the most rewarding. This is your final opportunity to repay the love and devotion that your dog has given to you during the happy times you have spent together. If you know what to expect during these remaining days, you will find the inner strength to cope with them.

As your old dog becomes more frail, its reliance on you will increase. Physical contact, and the message of love that it carries, is very important, so spend as much time as necessary gently stroking and cuddling your dog to let it know that you are there, and how much you care.

Making the decision

Sometimes the final decision is made for you. Death may come suddenly, a quick and merciful release from pain and suffering, ending a life from which all the joy has gone.

In most cases, though, there is no natural solution. You, the owner, will have to make the decision to authorise euthanasia.

ABOVE: Cataracts are common in old age – the eye will appear white in the centre – but most dogs can adapt. Surgery is often a good option.

1 Denial and depression

When you are confronted with the fact that your dog is at the end of its life, you will probably suffer from depression. This will often be subconscious, and not immediately apparent to those around you.

You may tell yourself that your vet has it wrong, or that things are not as bad as they seem. This reaction cushions your mind against the emotional blow it is experiencing.

2 Bargaining

In the human grieving process this involves offering some personal sacrifice if the loved one is spared. It is less likely to happen with your pet, but you may still say things to yourself such as 'if you get better I promise to take you back to your favourite park'.

3 Pain and anger

Your emotional pain evokes a feeling of anger that may be directed at somebody else, such as a close relative or even your veterinarian. It helps you to relieve your feeling of frustration, although this may be at somebody else's expense. Your anger may be directed at yourself, and emerge as a feeling of guilt: 'If only I hadn't...'

It is at this stage that the support of your veterinarian may be particularly helpful. Negative feelings are not constructive, and need to be replaced by positive thoughts such as 'I'm so glad that I did...'

4 Grief

By this stage anger and guilt have gone. You are faced with the grim reality that your dog is dead, and all that remains is an empty feeling. The less support you get at this stage, the longer that feeling will last.

If support doesn't come from your family or friends, then get it from another source, such as your veterinarian or a professional counsellor.

5 Acceptance and resolution

It will take time, on average about three to four months, but eventually your grieving will come to an end. Fond memories will replace grief, and appreciation will replace the sense of loss. You may even celebrate them by obtaining a new pet.

Our pets have a shorter life span than we do, and on average an owner will suffer the loss of a dearly loved pet

The decision may come easily, or you may find it very difficult. We witness death on television, videos and films many hundreds of times every year, yet most of us live in a society that does not cope well with dying, and are unprepared for it in 'real life'.

If there are children in your family, discuss the situation with them and allow them to express their feelings. Talk about the positive aspects of owning your dog, and explain that however good its health care may be, dogs have a much shorter life expectancy than we do.

The over-riding factor in your decision must be what is best for the dog, not for you or your family. That decision will probably be made with the help of your veterinarian, who can play an important role as counsellor and advisor. Vets and their staff understand your grief and sense of loss, but also know that they can end your dog's suffering in a humane way.

The grieving process: Grieving is a natural human reaction to the death of a much-loved person or animal. While society has long recognised the need to express it for humans, there has been less understanding of the need to express it for pets. This situation is changing, though, as we are learning more about the companion animal-human bond, which develops between owners and their pets. There are five well-documented stages in the grieving process.

TOP: A pet portrait can commemorate a dearly loved pet, as this old painting of an Affenpinscher demonstrates.

five times or more during a lifetime. Each time such a loss occurs, that owner will experience a feeling of grief. It doesn't get any easier the more often it happens, for each pet is an individual and the owner grieves individually for it.

Nevertheless, if you understand the stages of the grieving process and know how your family, friends and veterinarian can help, you should be able to deal with the loss with minimum of pain and maximum love.

The procedure: The procedure for euthanasia is similar to that used when a dog needs to be anaesthetised for an operation, except that in this case an overdose of anaesthetic is injected into the vein. There is no pain, and the dog loses consciousness within three to five seconds.

You may wish to be present during this procedure. Gently stroke your dog's head as the drug is injected, and spend a little time holding it after it has passed away. Or you may prefer not to witness the procedure, and say your last farewell afterwards. The choice will be yours.

At this point you will probably feel an overwhelming sense of loss. Don't be afraid to express it. Your veterinarian and the veterinary hospital staff who have assisted will understand that this is a natural reaction.

Burial or cremation: If you wish, your veterinarian will help you decide what to do next.

The ritual burial of pet remains is not unusual, and if you don't own a suitable area for this you may decide to purchase a burial plot at a pet cemetery. Prices vary, depending on the size of plot and the quality of casket. Some pet cemeteries include in their price a small inscribed granite marker, but you can also purchase a more elaborate memorial. If you choose cremation, a casket or urn containing the ashes can be returned to you.

You may wish to commission a monumental portrait, a long-lasting and durable photographic image that can be fixed outside on virtually any surface. Many pet cemeteries now provide for after-care of your pet's burial site. Some pet cemeteries offer family plots, pre-arranged burials, graveside services and daily cemetery visits.

Counselling: For some pet owners the lingering grief becomes intolerable. Seek help. You may want to call a traditional counselling service, or contact a veterinary teaching institution with social workers trained to counsel pet owners. Some counselling services are available around the clock. Once again, your veterinarian should be able to advise you.

ABOVE: Dogs left to sleep on hard surfaces or in cold conditions are more likely to suffer from arthritis when they are older. An early sign is stiffness when getting up.

BREEDING AND REPRODUCTION
A new member of the family

Puppies are adorable, but breeding from a family pet is not really advisable. It is far better to leave this to the experts who have proper facilities and plenty of time.

If you do have the time and are really committed, and one family member will be at home all day, then go ahead.

Contact the breeder of your bitch and let them choose a suitable mate. It is not acceptable to find any male of the same breed and use him as the sire as this may result in inferior puppies. It is important to select a male with the right genetic background, a good temperament, of good physical conformation and proven fertility.

The female reproductive cycle

Most bitches come into season (are in heat) every six months from the age of six to eight months. It is best to breed from the second or third heat. Each heat lasts for three weeks. Signs of heat are vulval swelling, followed by bleeding from the vulva. This lasts for about seven days and is followed by a straw-coloured discharge lasting for another week. There is no visible discharge during the third week. Bitches vary in the amount of discharge produced and some are so thorough in cleaning it up that their owners have difficulty in detecting the heat. Behaviour changes also occur during this time. The bitch becomes friendlier and may hold her tail down and to one side when patted near the tail base. She may also try to wander, and may urinate more frequently.

Male dogs can detect the scent of a bitch in heat from long distances and you may end up with dogs camped on your lawn for a while. It is important to keep the bitch safely enclosed during her heat and to take her out only on a leash.

The bitch is most fertile between the 10th and 14th days of heat, although there is individual variation. If the dog chosen as sire is close by then you can visit daily over this

TOP: When puppies are born they are covered by a membrane, which the bitch removes by licking.
ABOVE: A bitch prepares her whelping area: she may tear up paper or fabric to make a nest.

time and let nature take its course. However, if the sire is some distance away, it is useful to know exactly when the bitch will be fertile. This can be detected by a blood test, which measures serum progesterone levels. Your veterinarian can advise you on this.

Mating

In most cases, mating occurs reasonably rapidly after the dogs are introduced, especially if the stud dog (sire) is experienced. There are instances, though, where the dogs simply don't like each other and mating does not occur. Often this is because the bitch is dominant over the dog. If this happens, and you know that the bitch is definitely at the most fertile part of her cycle, it is better to find a different sire. Mating is usually done in the sire's home environment.

During mating, a gland on the male's penis becomes enlarged, entrapping the penis within the female tract for up to 20 minutes. During this time, the male may dismount and stand alongside or behind the bitch. Many owners become quite distressed seeing this for the first time. It is perfectly normal and the best thing to do is go and have a cup of tea for 20 minutes and leave them to it. This 'tie', as it is called, occurs in most but not all matings. If it does not occur, the mating may still be fertile.

Mismating

There are times when an unplanned mating occurs. If the bitch and the dog are tied together, do not forcibly separate them. Once natural separation has occurred, you must decide how to proceed. You have no way of knowing if the mating will be fertile.

If you are happy to let the bitch have the puppies resulting from this mating, proceed as discussed overleaf.

If you do not want the bitch to have the litter, and you wish to breed from her at a later date, your veterinarian can give her an injection to prevent pregnancy. There may be side effects from this, so talk to your vet about the pros and cons. If you don't want the bitch to have the litter, and you don't want to breed from her at a later date, you can have her spayed once her heat is finished.

ABOVE: The Border Collie, an excitable, boisterous and often aggressive breed, is safe and snug with her litter in her whelping box.

Care of the bitch

Before a bitch is mated, it important that she has had a recent health check and has had vaccinations within the last six months. This will help to ensure that the puppies are born with good levels of immunity to common diseases. It is also important that she is treated for roundworms prior to mating and during the pregnancy.

Applied products that are not absorbed but bind onto the lipid (oily) layer on the skin surface are safe to use. Check with your vet about the correct treatment.

During her pregnancy, the bitch should be familiarised with the whelping area. Ideally this should include a boxed-off bed area large enough for the bitch to stretch out fully lying on her side and for her to comfortably turn around in. It should be placed in a room or area that is quiet and away from the mainstream household traffic.

Put newspapers and old towels in the box for her to nest with. Place her in the area with a biscuit or one of her meals for a short while daily. If she is used to sleeping on a bed of her own, move this into the whelping box and encourage her to sleep there.

Whelping

The first stage of labour is indicated by restlessness, panting and pacing. This may continue for up to eight hours. The bitch will often tear up paper during this time and make a nest.

Eventually there will be obvious abdominal contractions and the bitch will get up and down frequently and will lick at her vulva. Within 20 to 60 minutes after the contractions begin, the first pup will be delivered. The puppies are covered with a membrane, which the bitch

The correct way in which to intervene in the birth process

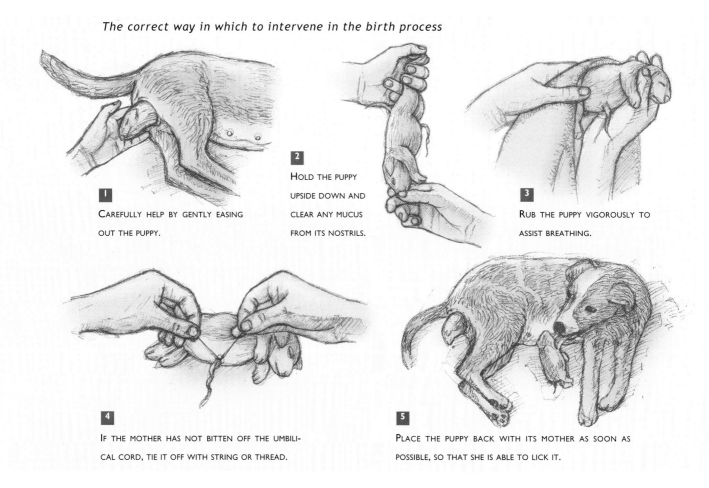

1 CAREFULLY HELP BY GENTLY EASING OUT THE PUPPY.

2 HOLD THE PUPPY UPSIDE DOWN AND CLEAR ANY MUCUS FROM ITS NOSTRILS.

3 RUB THE PUPPY VIGOROUSLY TO ASSIST BREATHING.

4 IF THE MOTHER HAS NOT BITTEN OFF THE UMBILICAL CORD, TIE IT OFF WITH STRING OR THREAD.

5 PLACE THE PUPPY BACK WITH ITS MOTHER AS SOON AS POSSIBLE, SO THAT SHE IS ABLE TO LICK IT.

moves by licking. They are attached via the umbilical cord to the placenta, which is delivered at the same time. The bitch chews through the umbilical cord and usually eats the placenta. She should be allowed to do this. The pups respond to her licking and nuzzling with high-pitched cries. They rapidly find the teats and begin to suckle.

If for some reason the bitch does not attend to one of her newborn puppies, it will be necessary to intervene (see the illustration on p122).

Have some clean, reasonably rough towels on hand. Make sure your hands are clean, and break the membrane over the puppies' mouth and nose. Try to clear fluid from its mouth with your finger and by holding it facing head down. Rub the puppy vigorously with the towel until it is obviously breathing and begins to cry. Place the puppy back in the nest near a teat. If the bitch has not chewed through the umbilical cord after 20 minutes, you should tie the cord off with thread and remove the placenta.

If at any stage the bitch strains and pushes for longer than half an hour without producing a puppy, call your vet.

Once the labour is over, offer the bitch some warm milk with glucose (one teaspoonful of glucose to one cup of milk). Leave her alone to rest and bond with the puppies.

It is better for one person only to be present during the whelping – your assistance may be needed, especially if it is a first litter. If you feel that your children would benefit by being present, insist that they are quiet and do not handle the newborn puppies.

feeding. If you are using a commercial diet, this should all be taken care of for you. There are special foods designed for the lactating bitch which are also suitable as food for the puppies when they start on solids. If you are feeding a home-cooked diet you will need to add calcium. This can be purchased in powder, liquid or tablet form from your veterinarian.

Most bitches prefer to be left undisturbed during the first two to three weeks after the labour. Take her out to toilet three or four times daily and change the nest twice daily while she is out on a toilet break – otherwise leave her to it unless she demands your company. Some bitches may show aggression at this time, and this is quite a problem (see p69, Maternal aggression).

Rearing the puppies

During the first two weeks of life the puppies spend most of their time suckling and sleeping. Feed the bitch up to four times daily during this time and ensure she has plenty of water available. Make sure that she has enough calcium in her diet while she is

ABOVE: The typical behaviour for four-day old puppies is sleeping and suckling.
TOP: A large litter may require additional feeds with a pet nursing bottle and pet milk formula.

If the bitch has produced a huge litter and cannot feed them all, you may need to supplement their feeding using a pet nursing bottle and pet milk replacement formula.

A reasonable litter size for a medium to large bitch is six to 10 pups. Anything over 10 may be a problem, although some mothers do manage to rear large numbers successfully without help. Check that all the puppies feed successfully and have full stomachs. If any of them seem thin and cry persistently, they are probably not getting sufficient food. If you are in any doubt, ask your veterinarian to evaluate the situation. Supplementary feeding of milk and formula is usually done in rotation with half the litter on the mother and half bottle fed at each feeding time (every two to three hours).

At 10 to 14 days of age the puppies' eyes will open and they will become more mobile and start to show early play behaviour. From two weeks onwards they should be offered solid food. Offer this four times daily. Baby cereals may be offered as well as canned puppy food or scraped meat (meat that has been frozen and is then grated and thawed). As previously mentioned, there are special commercial puppy-rearing foods available, which are generally a more suitable option.

The bitch may regurgitate food for the pups – this is normal behaviour and they may be allowed to eat what she produces.

Puppies should be treated for worms fortnightly from two weeks old, using tablets or a suspension. Worming is essential, as puppies become infected with worms before birth. No matter how well cared for, most bitches will carry the larval form of roundworms encysted in tissue somewhere in their bodies. When exposed to hormones during the pregnancy, these larvae are triggered to develop and migrate across the placenta and into the puppies. The bitch should also be wormed at two-weekly intervals while feeding the puppies because she will become re-infected by cleaning up after them (see pp84-90, Parasites)

From three weeks of age it is important that puppies have contact with people, as they need to become accustomed to handling. If you have visitors to the puppies at this time, take precautions to prevent transmission of viral diseases. Ask visitors to remove their shoes and to wash their hands before handling the puppies.

It is also important that from two to three weeks onwards, the puppies have access to an area outside the immediate nest in which to urinate and defecate. This area may be covered with newspaper, or it may be a sand tray. If outdoor temperatures are warm, they may be able to have access to a grassy area.

Puppies should go to new owners at seven to eight weeks of age. It is preferable that they should receive their

ABOVE: The correct way to pick up a puppy: be sure to support its body carefully.
TOP: Puppies learn from play – their mothers discipline them when they play too roughly and hurt their littermates.

they make positive responses to the approach of any new individual. This is an important time for them to have contact with people. They experience a fear phase at six weeks so this is not a good time for them to leave the litter. A second fear phase occurs at around 14 weeks. Puppies that have been well socialised prior to this will probably not show much change, but in some cases the change in response to new events or strange people is quite dramatic. If your puppy experiences this, you will need to help it by being patient and understanding.

Substrate preference, the selection of a specific area and type of substance for elimination purposes, develops at seven to eight weeks of age. This is a good time for puppies to go to a new home.

In a natural situation, pups would stay in a family group for six months and often longer. During this time there is constant change in the relative dominance of individuals. A pup that is dominant at eight weeks may not be at 12 weeks.

Puppies learn from play. If a puppy bites too hard, the victim will yelp and refuse to have anything to do with the offender. In this way they learn to control the intensity of their play. Their mother disciplines puppies that behave roughly. She will firmly place her mouth over a puppy's face to stop unacceptable behaviour, or she may push it onto its side and place a paw on its neck or shoulder. When a human is training a puppy these actions can be simulated to achieve a similar result.

first vaccination before they leave. Most vets will give a discount when vaccinating litters and it is very helpful to have had a thorough health check done on each one prior to sale.

Puppy social development

Puppies are born blind, deaf and with very limited mobility. Even at this early age they compete for access to their mother's teats. In large litters where not all the puppies can feed at one time, the strongest or most determined will do best.

During the first two weeks (neonatal period), senses of hearing, sight, smell, touch and taste develop rapidly.

At around 10 days the eyes and the ear canals open. By three weeks puppies begin to play. From three to five weeks

The social development of a puppy.

BIRTH	1–10 DAYS	3 WEEKS	5 WEEKS	6 WEEKS	7–8 WEEKS	14 WEEKS
Blind Deaf Limited mobility	Eyes open Ear canals open Begins to play	Positive response to the approach of any individual	Contact with people can now increase	First fear phase: do not remove from mother and littermates	Toilet training can begin; puppy is ready to go to a new home	Second fear phase: be patient and understanding

INDEX

Photographic Credits:

Animal Photography/RT Willbie: pp 24 top, 70 top, 71; Animal Photography/Sally Anne Thompson: pp 28, 34 top, 39, 57, 60, 75, 78, 97 top, 106 above, 115
85. Michael Brett: p 10 above. Bridgeman Art Library: p 13 top. Bruce Coleman Collection/Adriano Bacchella: p 15; Bruce Coleman Collection/Jane Burton: p 2;
Bruce Coleman Collection/Jeff Foott: p 12; Bruce Coleman Collection/Hans Reinhard: p 40. Cogis/Blat p 8; Cogis/Francais: pp 4, 10 top, 19, 20 above;
Cogis/Hermeline: pp 9,11 above, 31, 41, 56, 64; Cogis/Labat: pp 59, 62; Cogis/Lanceau: pp 6, 16, 20 top; Cogis/Vedie: p 21. John Daniels: pp 3, 11, 26 above,
29, 32 top left, 53, 65 top. Isabelle Francais: front cover main image, front cover top left, pp 11, 26 top, 34 above, 51, 63, 69. Gallo/Getty Images: front cover
below left; Gallo Images/Martin Harvey: p 13 above; Gallo Images/Tony Stone-David Tipling: p 14 above; Gallo Images/Ben Osborne: p 18. Graham Meadows:
back cover flap portraits, pp 14 top, 22 above, 27, 70 above, 118. Kelly Walsh: front cover flap, pp 42, 43, 44, 45, 46 top, 58 top, 59 above, 61, 62 above, 64
above, 95. Warren Photographic/Jane Burton: front cover second and third left, back cover, pp 1, 5, 17, 22 top, 23, 24 above, 30 top & above, 31, 32 top left, 33
above, 35, 36, 37, 38, 46 above, 47, 50, 52, 65 above, 72, 74, 76 top, 80, 81, 84, 85, 96, 97 above, 98, 99, 101, 102, 103, 104, 105, 106 top, 107, 108, 110, 111,
113, 114, 116, 117, 119, 120, 120 top, 123 above, 124, 125;Warren Photographic/Kim Taylor: p 48.